10 Essential Instructional Elements

for Students With Reading Difficulties

I would like to dedicate this book to my older brother, Dave Johnson, of Wausau, Wisconsin. He is the epitome of what an older brother should be.

10 Essential Instructional Elements

for Students With Reading Difficulties

A Brain-Friendly Approach

Andrew P. Johnson

FOR INFORMATION:

Corwin

A SAGE Company

2455 Teller Road

Thousand Oaks, California 91320

(800) 233-9936

www.corwin.com

SAGE Publications Ltd.

1 Oliver's Yard

55 City Road

London EC1Y 1SP

United Kingdom

SAGE Publications India Pvt. Ltd.

B 1/I 1 Mohan Cooperative Industrial Area

Mathura Road, New Delhi 110 044

India

SAGE Publications Asia-Pacific Pte. Ltd.

3 Church Street

#10-04 Samsung Hub

Singapore 049483

Senior Acquisitions Editor: Jessica Allan

Senior Associate Editor: Kimberly Greenberg

Editorial Assistants: Cesar Reyes and
Katie Crilley

Production Editor: Melanie Birdsall

Copy Editor: Grace Kluck

Typesetter: C&M Digitals (P) Ltd.

Proofreader: Sally Jaskold

Indexer: Amy Murphy

Cover Designer: Scott Van Atta

Marketing Manager: Jill Margulies

Printed in the United States of America

ISBN 978-1-4833-7377-5

This book is printed on acid-free paper.

SFI Certified Sourcing
www.sfiprogram.org
SFI-00453

15 16 17 18 19 10 9 8 7 6 5 4 3 2 1

Contents

SECTION III. 10 INSTRUCTIONAL ELEMENTS

Acknowledgments

Corwin gratefully acknowledges the contributions of the following reviewers:

Dolores M. Hennessy
Reading Specialist
Hill and Plain School
New Milford, CT

Natalie S. McAvoy
Reading Specialist/Interventionist
Elkhorn Area School District
Elkhorn, WI

Jeannie Thorp
Special Education Teacher
La Pine Elementary School
La Pine, OR

Joan Whoolery
Reading Specialist
Fairfax County Public Schools
Alexandria, VA

About the Author

 **Dr. Andrew P. Johnson** was a 1976 graduate of Grantsburg High School in Grantsburg, Wisconsin. He attended the University of Wisconsin, River Falls, where he graduated with a BS degree in music and speech-communication. After earning his elementary teaching licensure, he taught second grade in River Falls, Wisconsin, from 1983 to 1986. He went on to teach in elementary schools in the Twin Cities area and also spent three years working in the Grantsburg School District as a fifth-grade teacher and the Gifted Education coordinator.

He earned his PhD in literacy education from the University of Minnesota in 1997. He is currently working at Minnesota State University, Mankato, as a professor of literacy in the Department of Special Education where he specializes in literacy instruction for students with reading difficulties. He is the author of 10 books and numerous academic articles related to literacy, learning, teacher development, and the human condition.

He lives in North Mankato with his wife, Dr. Nancy Fitzsimons, and his dogs Mickey and Emmet.

Introduction

CONTEXT

In our society in this age one must be able to read in order to reach one's full potential. Not only do you need to know how to read, but you also must be able to do so efficiently and effectively. According to the National Institute of Literacy (part of the US Department of Education), 14% of US adults (or about 32 million) can't read, and 21% of US adults read below a fifth-grade level. This greatly impacts their ability to earn a living wage and adequately provide for themselves or a family.

Currently there are about 74 million children under the age of 18 living in the United States. The National Institute of Child Health and Human Development (NICHD) estimates that approximately 20% of them have trouble learning to read. This would be about 14 million children. Of these, 3% to 5% have significant reading difficulties (a severe reading disability). This would be between 2.2 and 3.7 million children. But even if one student was struggling to read, that would be too many, especially if that student was your own child. These students are twice as likely to drop out of high school when compared to their peers. As a result, they are more apt to be unemployed, underemployed, and incarcerated. This means they are far less able to contribute to society, provide for their families, spend money in our economy, and pay taxes. Thus, making sure all children learn to read is more than an educational issue; it's a social justice issue.

CODE FIRST OR MEANING FIRST

There are two basic theoretical perspectives related to reading instruction. These two perspectives used to be identified as phonics and whole language. Some may remember the reading wars of the late '80s and early '90s that pitted phonics against whole language. However, these terms are outdated and inaccurate today. Most teachers who identify themselves as whole language teachers use very explicit phonics instruction in their classrooms. In the same way, most teachers who advocate a phonics-first approach also strive to get students reading whole, complete, meaningful texts to the greatest extent possible. It is more accurate to say that differing theoretical perspectives are the following: a code-first approach based on a bottom-up model that has its basis in behavioral learning theory and a meaning-first approach based on an interactive model that has its basis in constructivism or cognitive learning theory.

Code First

The code-first approach to reading instruction places initial emphasis on decoding. Letter-identification skills of increasing complexity are taught in a specific order (scope and sequence) until students have sufficient command of phonological processes. This approach has been successfully used with many generations of students (including me). Lower-level letter sounds and other reading subskills are taught so that students will be able to engage in higher-level acts of comprehending whole, meaningful text. This reflects a bottom-up or phonological model of reading in which the processing of text is seen to move in a single direction, from letter sounds to words to meaning in part-to-whole fashion. Reading here is equated with sounding out words. In 1983, when I began teaching second grade in River Falls, Wisconsin, I could not imagine that there could possibly be any other way to teach students how to read.

Meaning First

The meaning-first approach to reading instruction places the emphasis on getting students engaged in whole, complete texts first, then teaching skills within that meaningful context. Reading here is defined not as sounding out words but as creating meaning with print. Reading is seen as both a top-down and bottom-up process. This reflects an interactive model of reading. Higher-level cognitive processes interact with lower-level letter identification skills to create meaning during the act of reading. I call this a neurocognitive model because of the importance of both neurological functions and cognitive structures in creating meaning with print. Explicit instruction is used to teach phonics as well as other word identification skills. However, this instruction takes place in the context of whole, meaningful text to the greatest extent possible so that students are able to simultaneously develop the ability to use higher-level processes as well as lower-level skills.

Top Down

What about a top-down model of reading? Here, higher-level cognitive structures and processes would be used almost exclusively to identify words. Skills instruction of any kind would be minimal. Whole language teaching is often mischaracterized as a purely top-down approach; however, in my experience, very few people (if any) subscribe to a purely top-down approach to reading instruction. Most whole language teachers and scholars believe in very direct and explicit phonics instruction. It's not the "what" of phonics instruction that is in question, it's the "how" and "how much" of phonics instruction.

TOOLS IN YOUR TEACHING TOOLBOX

The thumbnail sketches presented above are by no means completely descriptive of the two general approaches to reading instruction. They are meant simply to provide context for the chapters that follow. As to which one is the "correct" approach, there will always be well-informed people of good character on both sides of this issue. I subscribe to a meaning-first approach based on the neurocognitive model of reading. From my perspective, a vast array of research from many different fields clearly points to the neurocognitive model of reading. However, I recognize that others disagree. Regardless of your theoretical perspective, the strategies presented in this book can be used to enable you to help students develop their ability to create meaning with print. That said, this book does not offer a specific method for reading instruction. It does not provide a recipe for reading interventions. Rather, it contains a variety of teaching strategies and activities that you can use to help struggling readers.

My goal with this book is to provide an array of tools for your teaching toolbox. Like any tool, the effectiveness of each strategy is dependent on how it is used. Thus, I recommend that all strategies presented in this book, like any strategy or tool, be adopted and adapted to fit your particular teaching situation and to meet the needs of your students. One last thing: The strategies here are designed for and have been used with students from kindergarten through higher education. Again, adopt and adapt. A very important scientific principle is this: If it works, do more of it. If it doesn't work, do less of it.

AUDIENCE

This book was initially written to be a professional-development book for teachers. For this purpose, I recommend creating book clubs or professional-development discussion groups based on this book. Ideally, these groups would meet every two weeks to share the strategies you implemented, how you implemented them, and how they work. If you go to my website (www.OPDT-Johnson.com), you'll find directions for discussion groups, specific discussion group questions, and activities for each chapter. As well, I will be creating online forums for these types of professional-development discussion groups.

I have also found this book to be particularly well suited for use in my literacy-methods courses at Minnesota State University, Mankato, where I teach (bias noted). To make this book more accessible to all, I've tried to keep the chapters short and the language less formal.

Finally, with my audience in mind, I've tried to keep citations to a minimum; however, there are some chapters that describe important theoretical perspectives that tend to generate many questions. You will find these chapters to be heavily cited.

Section I

Understanding the Reading Process

1

Creating Meaning With Print

The Neurocognitive Model

Reading is creating meaning with print.

Over the course of the next three chapters, I will describe the process of reading first from a neurological perspective and then from a cognitive perspective. Understanding the process our brains use to create meaning with text will enable you to design and plan effective reading instruction. As stated in the Introduction, the content contained in these first chapters tends to generate questions and sometimes even controversy. Thus, I have included many more reference citations in these first chapters than I do in later chapters.

UNDERSTANDING READING

The Phonological Processing Model of Reading

The *phonological processing model* (described briefly in the Introduction) defines reading as simply sounding out words. According to this model, reading is a bottom-up process. Here information flows one way, from the page (the bottom) through the eyes, to the thalamus, and up to the higher regions of the brain or the cortex (the top) (Figure 1.1). According to this model, our eyeballs move in a straight line from left to right along the page as we perceive, and then process each individual letter in our working memory. Each letter is then converted into a sound, the sounds are pasted together to form words, each word is put into a sentence, and each sentence is then put in the context of a greater idea and comprehended. However, that's a whole lot of small moving parts to try to assemble in working memory in the microseconds available to us as we read words and sentences.

Based on the phonological processing model, students with reading disabilities are often given a lot of sounding-out instruction with the assumption that this will help them learn to read. These types of phonics-based programs may improve students' ability to sound out words in isolation, but by themselves, they tend to be minimally effective (Johannessen & McCann, 2009; Strauss, 2011).

Figure 1.1   Bottom-Up View of Reading

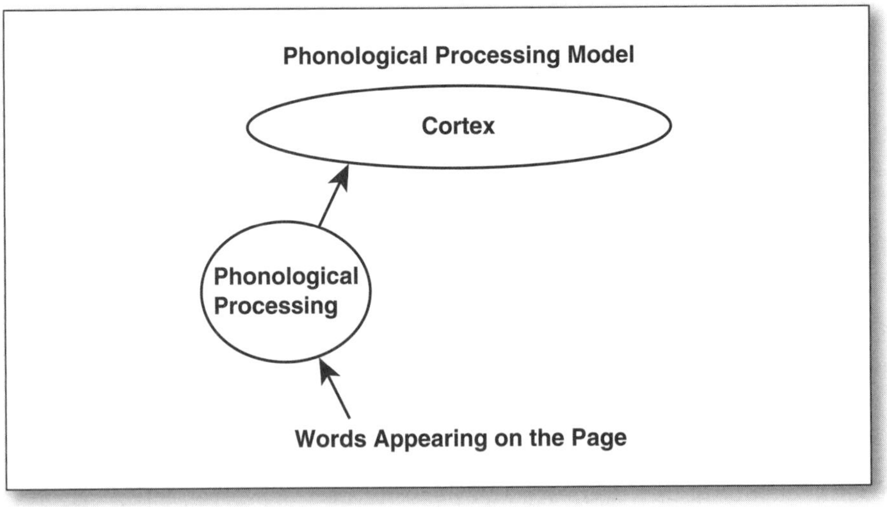

Phonological Processing Model

Cortex

Phonological Processing

Words Appearing on the Page

The Neurocognitive Model of Reading

The *interactive* or *neurocognitive model* defines reading as creating meaning with print. Sounding out words is seen as only part of the process of creating meaning with print. To illustrate, when you hear somebody speak, you perceive the individual sounds of each word and the individual words, but listening in this sense is different from perceiving individual sounds or putting sounds together to form words. To listen here is to ascribe meaning to the message. You pay minimal attention to the individual sounds and words and instead focus on meaning or what these are pointing you toward. Indeed, the sounds and words carry little meaning by themselves. Instead, these are always found within a meaningful context. As you listen, you use semantics (meaning or context), along with syntax (word order and grammar), and background knowledge (schemata) to understand what the speaker is trying to tell you.

Reading is much the same. We use what's in our head along with the little squiggly shapes appearing on the page to create meaning. Expert readers do not attend to every letter (Paulson & Freeman, 2003; Weaver, 2009); instead, they use minimal letter clues along with context (semantics), the information in our heads (schemata), and syntax to create meaning with print (Binder, Duffy, & Rayner, 2001; Hruby & Goswami, 2013; Rayner & Well, 1996). Right now, as you are reading this page, you are not processing each individual letter. Your eyeballs are actually stopping to focus or fixate on approximately 85% of the content words and approximately 35% of the function words (Rayner, Juhasz, & Pollatestk, 2007). Your eyeballs are making small backward movements (regressions) to refocus on certain content words that may be less familiar to you as well.

Creating Meaning With Print

To illustrate further, take a minute to read the text in Figure 1.2. Notice the difference between reading this and the text in the preceding paragraph. Below your reading was most likely much slower and choppier, your eyeballs made more fixations and regressions, you needed to stop to process and review individual letters, and you sounded out each part of the big words before you put them together. In essence, your reading was very much like that of a struggling reader. And, unless you know Latin, you were not creating meaning with print. Thus, you were unable to use syntax and semantics to try to make sense of this.

Figure 1.2   Sound This Out

Mea no mucius omittam lobortis, ex eam copiosae vivendum disputando. An est amet inciderint, ne tale etiam adolescens vel, idque postea neglegentur vix eu. Eius nemore ad vel, his veritus eleifend no. Tantas periculis maiestatis sit ne, id eum modo assueverit dissentiet, dicat quaerendum no pro. Id nonumes luptatum percipitur nec, at nec maiorum expetenda abhorreant, bonorum luptatum his an.

READING: A NEUROLOGICAL PERSPECTIVE

We read with our brain. As we read, our brain is constantly reaching out to fill in the blanks or predict the meanings of words in the sentences we are reading (Hawkins, 2004; Paulson & Goodman, 2008). Words are verified using three cueing systems: (a) semantic, (b) syntactic, and (c) grapho-phonetic (Anderson, 2013; Hruby & Goswami, 2013; Strauss, 2011) (Figure 1.3).

Figure 1.3   Three Cueing Systems

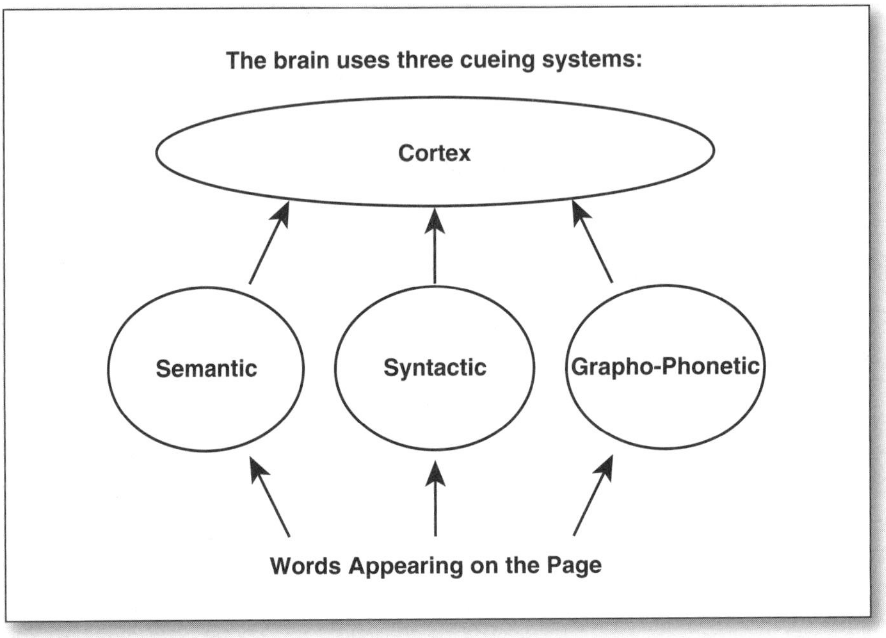

The Three Cueing Systems

1. Semantic

The semantic cueing system is the most efficient of the three in terms of speed and space required in working memory to recognize words. Semantics refers to meaning. As you read, you use context and background knowledge to identify words and figure out what the next word might be. For example:

The monkey ate a _ _ _ _ _ _.

You most likely know what the next word is in the sentence above. As your brain read the sentence, it focused on the words "monkey" and "ate." This narrowed the possibilities of the word to something monkeys eat. Based on your knowledge of monkey stereotypes, cartoons, and Tarzan movies, you most likely inserted the word "banana." If you did not immediately insert the word "banana," your brain would have then used the first letter to figure it out. If the word "banana" fit with what went before and after you would have continued. We use the knowledge in our head to predict meanings and confirm meanings or make revisions during the reading process.

The monkey ate a b _ _ _ _ _.

2. Syntactic

Syntax has to do with the grammatical structure of the language. As your brain reads, you also use your knowledge of grammar, sentence structure, word order, tense and plurality, prefixes and suffixes, nouns and verbs, and function words (prepositions, pronouns, etc.) to identify words. This is the second most efficient cueing system.

For example, in the monkey sentence above you focused on the word "monkey" (noun) and "ate" (verb). Your brain knew the missing word had to be a noun of some sort. Using syntax together with semantics you were able to easily fill in the missing word. This is how reading works. Your brain works holistically to create meaning with print.

Let me illustrate the idea of syntax further. Read the short nonsense story in Figure 1.4 on the next page and answer the comprehension questions. Even though it is meaningless, you will discover that you can still answer all the questions simply by examining the syntax. (The answers are at the end of this chapter.)

3. Grapho-Phonetic

"Grapho" refers to symbols; "phono" refers to sounds. The grapho-phonetic cueing system uses letter sounds to predict what the next word might be. Of the three cueing systems, this one is the least efficient. Why? Because it focuses on individual letters and letter patterns instead of words and ideas. As you will see in Chapter 3, your working memory has very limited capacity. You can try to stuff a few letters in there, a few words, or a few ideas, but which would be the most efficient in terms of creating meaning with print? An idea is much bigger than a letter. There are far more things contained in an idea than in a letter.

Figure 1.4   Using Syntax to Create Meaning

A Plumple for Luffy

Flam was very nurff. She had smacken Luffy's plumple. She didn't flink a fushat for him. So, she clepped a plumple for him. She had just atturd the flecker when he ralfed in the smarcker.

"Scrad flammet!" Flam ressed.

Luffy ressed, "That's a smerrest plumple. But my plumple is on Klacky. Murd is Seeland."

"In that relt," ressed Flam, "I won't flink your fushat until Klacky."

Comprehension Questions

1. Why was Flam nurff?

2. What did Flam clepp?

3. Who ralfed in the smarcker when Flam clepped the plumple?

4. What did Flam do to the flecker?

5. Why didn't Flam flink Luffy's fushat?

Source: Based on an example from Sandra Wilde's book, *Miscue Analysis Made Easy* (2000).

The Relative Unimportance of Letters

Letters are not nearly as important as you might think. Figure 1.5 contains a short email message that I sent to students in one of my literacy classes at Minnesota State University, Mankato. I kept the first and last letters the same but scrambled up the inside ones. Are you able to create meaning? How is this possible?

Figure 1.5   Scrambled Inside Letters

I tnihk tihs is a wnuerdfol casls. You are gniog to be geart scapeil eatoucidn tahecres. You are all tlury aaingzmg hamun bgenis. You are aslo good ppoel.

Let me again demonstrate the relative unimportance of letters. Figure 1.6 is a short fairy tale. All the vowels except the initial vowels have been removed. Can you still create meaning with this text? How is this possible?

Figure 1.6   Text With All but the Initial Vowels Removed

Onc upn a tm thr ws a hndsm prnc. H lvd in a cstle. On dy an evl wzrd cm and trnd h int a frg. Th princ crd ot, "Hlp m!"
A btfl prncss cm t th cstl. Sh kssd hm on th lps. H trnd bck int a prnc. Thy lvd hppl vr aftr.

Which are the more unimportant, vowels or consonants? I will let you be the judge. Compare the top sentence, which contains only vowels, with the bottom sentence, which contains only consonants, in Figure 1.7. They are both the same sentence. Which one enables you to best create meaning? Based on this, how much time should we spend on diagraphs, diphthongs, magic *e* syllables, vowel pairs, controlled *r* syllables, and the schwa sound?

Figure 1.7   Vowels vs. Consonants

Vowels only: E ee a ae ae e e ooa ea i e. e ae a ea uaea.

Consonants only: Th Grn By Pckrs r th bst ftbll tm n th NFL. Thy hv a grt qrtrbck.

THE NEUROCOGNITIVE PROCESSES

So here is how it all works: As visual data is taken in from the eyes, it moves to the relay station in the brain called the thalamus. All three cueing systems are then used to make sense of this data before it moves to the cortex (see Figure 1.8). The cortex is the part of the brain responsible for higher-level thinking and memory. A system here is not a particular location or part of the brain but a series of interconnected parts or regions (Fischer, Immordino-Yang, & Waber 2007; Xu et al., 2005).

But wait . . . as stated above, information does not flow just one way from the page to the thalamus and up to the cortex. Brain imaging research shows that as we process data taken in by the various senses, information also flows from the cortex down to the thalamus

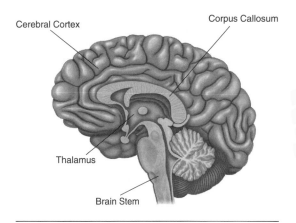

Cerebral Cortex

Corpus Callosum

Thalamus

Brain Stem

Source: ©iStockphoto.com/alexluengo

(Engel, Fries, & Singer, 2001; Hawkins, 2004; Hruby, 2009; Koch, 2004). As a matter of fact, there is almost 10 times more information flowing down from the cortex to the thalamus than up from the thalamus to the cortex (Alitto & Usrey, 2003; Destexhe, 2000; Gilbert & Sigman, 2007; Koch, 2004; Sherman & Guillery, 2004; Strauss, 2011) (Figure 1.8). This means that higher structures of the brain (those involved in thought and reasoning) control or influence the lower structures during the act of processing visual information (Ducket, 2008; Gilbert & Sigman, 2007; Hawkins, 2004).

Figure 1.8   Information Flow: Cortex to Thalamus to Cortex

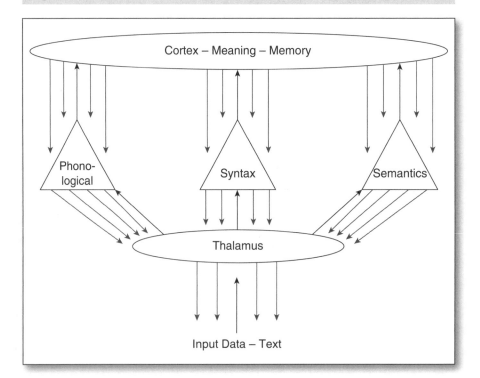

Speed and Efficiency

So what does this mean? We perceive and interpret reality (including text) in terms of the information, images, and patterns stored in our cortex (Engel, Fries, & Singer, 2001; Siegel, 2007). These various forms of data are used to reach out and make predictions about what we are about to experience or encounter (Hawkins, 2004; Schwartz & Begley, 2002). Sense data is then used to confirm or revise these predictions and to encode our current version of reality. As well, we perceive only the salient aspects of any situation and use relevant information in our cortex to fill in the blanks (Baars & Gage, 2007). Our brains have evolved to operate this way for the purpose of speed and efficiency (LeDoux, 1996).

When used to create meaning with print, this process has been described as a psycholinguistic guessing game (Goodman, 1986). However, this phrase has been misunderstood and misinterpreted by some. It does not mean to imply that we randomly guess at words during the act of reading or that we teach children to guess at words. Rather, it means that cognitive efficiency and accuracy are achieved when the knowledge structures and higher-level processes are used to make sense of incoming data. In terms of reading, effective readers use the information in their head along with semantic and syntactic information to make sense of what's on the page.

The Meaninglessness of Individual Words

If you are locked into the phonological model and believe that reading is simply sounding out words, the three-cueing systems model will make no sense. Much of the research used to support the phonological model of reading is based on the assumption that reading is sounding out words (Hruby, 2009; Schulz et al., 2008; Strauss, Goodman, & Paulson, 2009). These studies commonly asked students to identify single words or nonsense words apart from any meaningful context. However, rarely (if ever) do we encounter single words in isolation. Even signs or labels that contain single words are seen in some context. For example, stop signs, signs for fast-food restaurants, or product labels are all encountered in a meaningful context. Indeed, about the only time we ever encounter individual words outside of a meaningful context is when we ask students to read lists of words or nonsense words for some type of reading test.

Research to support the three-cueing systems model comes from a variety of areas including eye movement studies (Binder, Duffy, & Rayner, 2001; Paulson & Goodman, 2008; Rayner & Well,

1996), schema studies in cognitive psychology (Anderson, 2013; Andersson & Barnitz, 1984; McVee, Dunsmore, & Gauelek, 2013), priming studies in psycholinguistics and cognitive psychology (Chernove, 1979; Münte, Heinze, & Mangun, 1993; Osterhout & Holcomb, 1992; Trueswell, 1996), miscue analysis studies (Goodman & Goodman, 2013), various brain imaging studies (Flegal, Marin-Gutierrex, Ragland, & Ranganath, 2014; Friederici & Kotz, 2003; Friederici & Weissenborn, 2007; Hogoort, 2003; Kuperberg, 2007; Poldrack et al., 1999; Sakai, Noguchi, Takeuchi, & Watanabe, 2002; Schulz et al., 2008; Van Berkum, Hagoort, & Brown, 1999), and studies related to reading instruction (Clay 1991; Isakson & Miller, 1976; Kennedy & Weener, 1974; Weaver, 1979). This list of studies and research reviews is a sampling and by no means comprehensive. It does, in my view, provide overwhelming support for the three-cueing systems model.

Last Word

The last thing to mention about the three-cueing systems model described above is that it is not an approach or a method of reading instruction. It's a model that describes how the brain identifies words during the act of creating meaning with print. To help all readers reach their full reading potential, all three cueing systems must be developed. The chapters that follow will present a variety of strategies for doing just this.

Answers

Figure 1.4 Comprehension Questions:

1. Why was Flam nurff?

   Because she had smacken Luffy's plumple.

2. What did Flam clepp?

   A plumple.

3. Who ralfed in the smarcker when Flam clepped the plumple?
   Luffy.

4. What did Flam do to the flecker?

   She atturd it.

5. Why didn't Flam flink Luffy's fushat?

Because his plumple was on Klacky.

Figure 1.5:

I think this is a wonderful class. You are going to be great special education teachers. You are all truly amazing human beings. You are also good people.

Figure 1.6:

Once upon a time there was a handsome prince. He lived in a castle. One day an evil wizard came and turned him into a frog. The prince cried out, "Help me!"

A beautiful princess came to the castle. She kissed him on the lips. He turned back into a prince. They lived happily ever after.

Figure 1.7:

The Green Bay Packers are the best football team in the NFL. They have a great quarterback.

2

Eye Movement and Neural Pathways

Reading: It's all about the neurons.

EYE MOVEMENT DURING READING

The section below examines how your eyes function while creating meaning with print.

Your Dancing Eyeballs

As described briefly in the last chapter, when you read sentences your eyeballs do not move across the page from left to right in a steady line processing each letter and looking at each word in an orderly fashion. Rather, eye movement studies show that your eyes move unevenly while reading, skipping some words, stopping on others, and going back to review words (Paulson & Goodman, 2008; Rayner, 2009). The small, rapid, jerky movements or skips that your eyes make during reading are called *saccades*. The average saccade length is 7 to 9 letter spaces. Stopping on a word is called a *fixation*. The average duration of a fixation is 225 to 250 milliseconds. Going back for a repeated fixation is called a *regression*.

Figure 2.1 illustrates how your eyeballs move across the page as you are reading. The dots represent fixations or stopping points, and the line represents the path your eyes take. When you are reading it only appears that your eyes are moving in a straight, steady line because your brain is striving to create meaning and produce complete sentences and ideas.

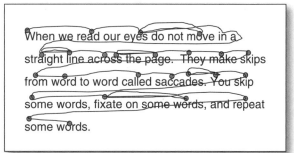

Figure 2.1   Eye Movement

As stated in the last chapter, you fixate on approximately 85% of the content words and 35% of the function words as you read. This would be only 60% of the total words. With unfamiliar material there are more fixations, with familiar material there are you fewer. This means that your eyes generally skip right over 40% of the words you read. You're doing it right now. It only appears that you're processing individual letters and words because your brain is filling in the blanks.

To illustrate how your brain fills in the blanks, look quickly at Figure 2.2. Even though you have only some of the visual data, you perceive complete shapes here. This is because your brain automatically completes the picture. This same process occurs as you read. Based on partial data, your brain creates order by filling in the blanks.

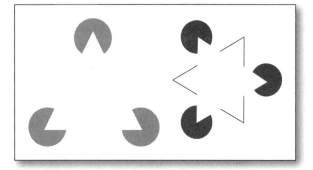

Figure 2.2   Our Brain Fills in the Blanks

So how do your eyes know which words to skip, fixate, or review? Higher-level cortical processes are actually directing your eyes where to fixate, which words to skip, and the number and types of regressions to make as you are reading (Ducket, 2008; Rayner, Juhasz, & Pollatsek, 2007; Rayner, Liversedge, White, & Vergilino-Perez, 2003; Rayner & Well, 1996).

Do cognitive processes drive the eyes in reading? At some level, we would have thought that the answer to this question has already been conclusively answered in the affirmative. Rayner

(1998) identified well over 100 published articles showing some influence of cognitive processing on eye fixation and eye movement. (Rayner, Juhasz, & Pollatsek, 2007, p. 93)

Scanner

Your eyes need to move in order to paint the picture of reality on the canvas of your brain. Try this experiment: Find a spot on the wall or a letter on the page. Stare at it without moving your eyeballs. Keep them perfectly still (something that's hard to do). You'll find that the spot or letter begins to blur and fade. To maintain a clear picture your eyes needs to move back and forth over the object in order to pick up light patterns. In this way they act very much like the scanners at the grocery store.

> **Experiment.** Look at a nonmoving object or a picture. As you do, notice the path your eyes take. They are making slight movements, going back and forth, up and down, creating patterns for the brain to interpret. In this sense, you are making miniscans of the reality in front of you, whether you are reading a book or observing reality.
>
> Now read a sentence on this page. Notice how your eyeballs make slight movements, up and down, back and forth. Eye movement helps to create the patterns that imprint on the brain. Again, the brain is not a minicamera that replicates reality; rather, the brain is an artist that creates pictures based on the sense patterns it receives and the information you already have. Put another way, our brains do not replicate reality; they interpret reality based on perceived data. And each person's interpretation of reality is a little bit different.

Perception

Your eye has three visual regions available during reading: foveal, parafoveal, and peripheral (see Figure 2.3). The *foveal* takes up only 1% to 2% of your total vision. This is the point of fixation where you are able to see clearly and process details. You can take in only about three to six letters here. The *parafoveal* is the region directly surrounding the foveal region. Here you are able to take in about 24 to 30 letters, however, not very clearly. In this region you can identify gross shapes but without some sort of context, the strings of letters are indistinguishable. The *peripheral* region is everything else. Here you are able to perceive only gross shapes.

So with this very small in-focus viewing area how is it possible for anybody to read more than 10 words per minute? Efficient readers are able to read quickly because of the top-down flow of information (Hawkins, 2004). Again, when we read, we use the information in our head (schemata) along with the context of what we are reading (semantics) and the syntax of the sentences to make predictions about the upcoming text (Paulson, 2008). These predictions enable us to make sense of the semiblurred letters found in the parafoveal regions and to recognize words. Again, efficient readers don't process every letter in a word and they don't fixate on every word in a sentence; rather, they recognize words using semantics and syntax and minimal letter clues. Because we're creating meaning with print, our brain only tricks us into thinking we have looked at every letter in every word.

Figure 2.3   Foveal, Parafoveal, and Peripheral Regions

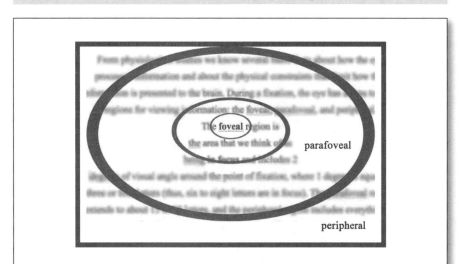

UNDERSTANDING OUR LEARNING ORGAN

The brain is our learning organ. There are three main parts of the human brain: the brain stem, the cerebellum, and the cerebrum. The *brain stem*, sometimes called the reptilian brain or the lower brain, is the oldest most primitive part of the human brain. It regulates our life support systems and things within our body that do not take conscious thought.

The *cerebellum* is a small part of the brain that plays an important role in motor control. It takes input from other parts of the brain, the spinal cord, and sensory receptors in order to coordinate the movements of the muscles and skeleton.

The *cerebrum* is the largest part of the brain. It's covered by a thin layer called the *cerebral cortex* (Figure 2.4). This is responsible for the higher-cognitive functions such as thinking, reasoning, imagination, decision making, and problem solving. The cerebral cortex is divided into four sections called lobes. Each lobe is associated with certain types of thinking:

- **Frontal Lobe.** Reasoning, decision making, emotions, problem solving, and parts of speech.
- **Parietal Lobe.** Movement, perception of stimuli, taste, recognition, and orientation.
- **Occipital Lobe.** Visual processing.
- **Temporal Lobe.** Memory, speech, and perception and recognition of auditory stimuli.

Figure 2.4   The Brain

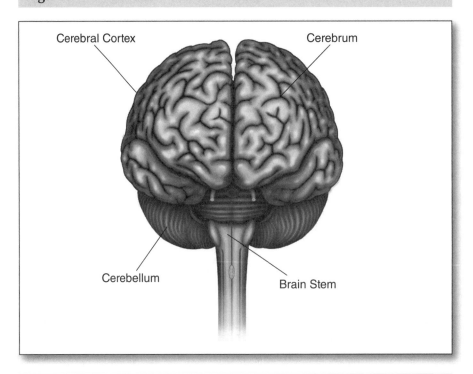

Source: ©iStockphoto.com/alexluengo

An Integrated Whole

There are two halves or hemispheres to the brain that are connected by the *corpus callosum*. Each side of the brain has some specialization; however, the brain works holistically. That is, the two sides work as an integrated whole, communicating back and forth. Thus, while people may be better able to process certain types of data, there is no such thing as left-brained or right-brained people. In the same way, while there are certain areas of the brain that seem to specialize in certain types of tasks, there are no specific parts that are totally responsible for any one function. Instead, thinking is distributed across many areas of the brain. And, when it comes to reading, the brain uses a variety of interconnected parts or systems to create meaning with print (Fischer, Immordino-Yang, & Waber, 2007; Hruby & Goswami, 2013; Xu et al., 2005). (Remember that reading is different from sounding out words.)

Creating Neural Networks

Most of what we call thinking and learning occurs in the cerebrum, specifically the cerebral cortex where there are billions of brain cells called *neurons* (Figure 2.5). Each neuron is like a minicomputer that transmits and receives electrochemical signals in the form of nerve impulses. Each neuron can send up to 50,000 messages per minute. Multiply this by the 100 to 200 billion neurons in our brains, and you begin to understand the power of this human-brain computing device.

From a purely neurological perspective, learning of any kind is a matter of creating neural networks and strengthening neural pathways. When stimuli in the external world are perceived, relevant sense organs send signals to various parts of our brain where neurons are stimulated. (Neurons can also be stimulated by other neurons as well. For example, the very act of thinking about something stimulates neurons and related neurons.) Once

Figure 2.5   Neurons

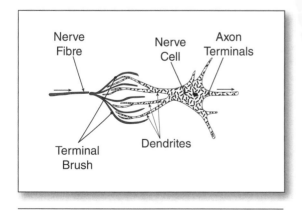

Source: Courtesy of www.clipart.com.

stimulated, a signal in the form of an electrical impulse is sent down a long fiber of the individual neuron called an *axon* (Figure 2.6). At the end of the axon, there is a gap that separates the neurons called a *synapse*. Here the electrical impulse triggers a chemical release (*neurotransmitter*) that crosses the gap. The neurotransmitters are picked up on the other side of the gap by *neuroreceptors* found at the end of a shorter, branching fiber called a *dendrite*. The dendrite brings the signal up to the new neuron. The signal then continues its journey down the axon to the next neuron and beyond.

Stimulated neurons automatically send and receive messages to and from all the surrounding or related neurons. As new neurons become linked up, *neural pathways* are created, existing pathways are strengthened, and more sophisticated webs or *neural networks* are formed (Figure 2.7). These neural networks facilitate the processing of new and related information. In other words, learning and experiencing new things creates new and more expansive neural networks,

Figure 2.6   Axon and Dendrites

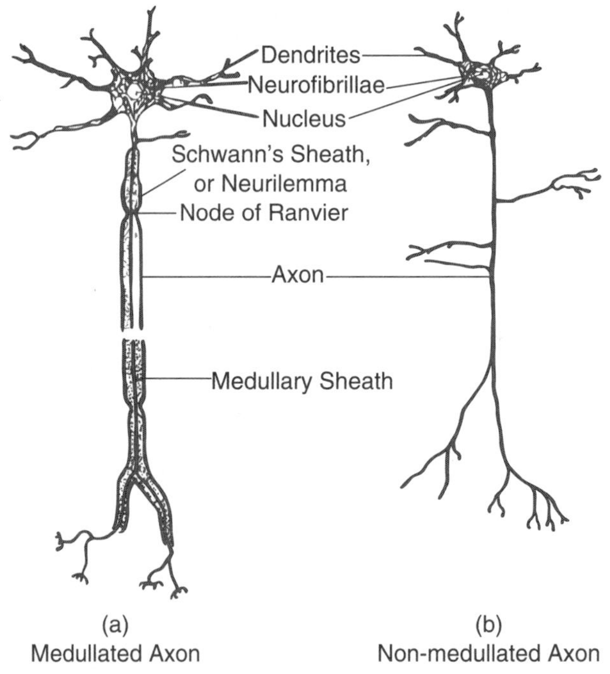

Dendrites
Neurofibrillae
Nucleus
Schwann's Sheath, or Neurilemma
Node of Ranvier
Axon
Medullary Sheath

(a)
Medullated Axon

(b)
Non-medullated Axon

Source: Courtesy of www.clipart.com.

making it easier to make connections with other new and related information and experiences. These neural networks represent the information in the head that's used to make sense of the information on the page during the process of reading. Thus, learning begets more learning. The more we learn, the easier it becomes to learn more.

Figure 2.7   Neural Network

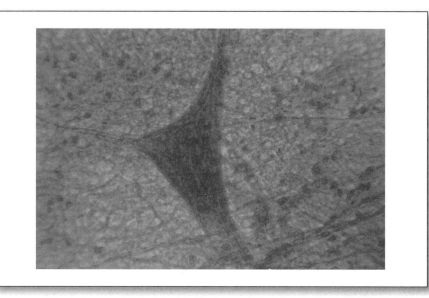

Source: Thinkstock/Comstock Images.

We Create Our Own Reality

At birth, billions of neurons exist in our brain like a gigantic dot-to-dot picture (Figure 2.8), but for the most part the dots are not connected, and there are no preconceived pictures. As we begin receiving various stimuli from the physical environment, neurons fire and become connected with other neurons to form intercommunicating neural networks. The dots begin to connect and form our ever-evolving picture of reality. As stated above, these neural networks help us to perceive and process new information from the world around us. Thus, how we interpret and perceive reality is determined by our past experiences. Since each person's neural networks are unique to that person and his or her experiences, each person has a slightly different picture of reality. This means that there can be no such thing as a

Figure 2.8 A Giant Dot-to-Dot Picture

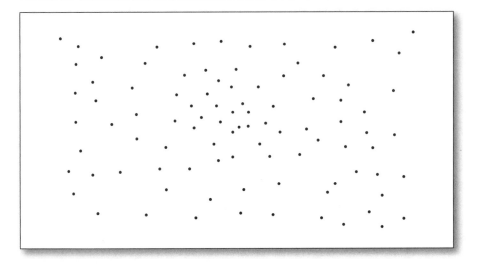

totally objective view of reality since even the most objective accounts of data are still subjected to a very subjective interpretation.

As we act upon the world, the world in turn acts upon us in the form of new neural pathways and neural networks. And as you can see, learning actually changes the physical structure of the brain as new neural networks are formed. The term for this is *neuroplasticity.* It refers to the brain's ability to organize and reorganize itself by forming new neural connections throughout one's life.

Right now you are reading about the human brain. You most likely have had some exposure to information related to this. These related neural networks are sending mild electrochemical impulses back and forth. As you pick up new bits of information from this chapter, these networks connect with other neurons and expand. The dot-to-dot picture becomes more detailed with more lines connecting to more dots. And as you see how one thing is associated with another, connections between other neural networks are formed. And as you continue to visit this network with new and related bits of information, the pathways between neurons become wider as more neurons are connected.

As you are striving to make sense of this chapter and as you are connecting new information to known information and your own experiences, your brain is changing. This change will make comprehending a little bit easier the next time you read something about learning and the brain.

Last Word

I will end this chapter with one important teaching tip: Struggling readers need lots of reading practice to become better readers. The vast majority of students who are struggling readers already know how to read. They understand the process of putting sounds to letters, creating words and such. The problem for most struggling readers is that they can't read very well. There's no question that some explicit, direct instruction is needed, but what these students need most is reading practice. It's hard to learn or to become better at anything new if you aren't able to practice. Too often, very few opportunities for reading practice are given to struggling students. Just as musicians practice scales and athletes spend countless hours practicing various aspects of their sport; readers need daily practice in order to automatically recognize words and phrases as they are reading. Musicians and athletes practice in order to strengthen neural pathways and develop neural networks. Reading is the same. It's all about the neurons.

3

Understanding Reading From a Cognitive Perspective

We use knowledge stored in long-term memory to help us understand and make sense of the world we live in.

THE DIFFERENCE BETWEEN BRAIN AND MIND

The difference between brain and mind is this: Our brain is the actual physical organ, the blob of jiggling, gray jelly in our cranium. Our mind is an accumulation of the thinking, feeling, and consciousness that arise from that blob of jelly. It is the mind that makes us human and it includes attention, thoughts, reasoning, creativity, will, memory, intuition, and imagination. Here's an analogy: The brain is the engine in the car. The mind is the car with a person in it driving down the road. Neuroscience studies the brain. Cognitive science or cognitive psychology studies the mind.

In the last chapter, we used neuroscience to help us understand the physical properties and functioning of the brain during the process of reading. In this chapter, we will use cognitive learning theory, a derivative of cognitive psychology, to help us understand how our mind functions during the process of reading. Both of these perspectives can be used to help inform our teaching practice.

THE INFORMATION PROCESSING MODEL

The information processing model, sometimes called the standard memory model, is central to understanding cognitive learning theory (Eggen & Kauchak, 2007). It describes how we take in information as well as how we analyze, organize, store, and retrieve it (Figure 3.1).

Perception—Sensory Register—Sense Memory

Stimuli are the sense data we encounter in the form of sights, sounds, smell, feel, and taste. *Perception* is the detection of stimuli through our five senses. We are bombarded with millions of stimuli every day. However, if we were to attend to all the stimuli we encountered, we'd soon be overwhelmed. Thus, we make decisions about which stimuli we will attend to.

Attention refers to the choices we make about which perceived stimuli to allow into consciousness in order to assign meaning. In any given situation, you decide which particular stimuli to focus on. Right now as you're reading this text, you are choosing to attend to the visual stimuli in front of you (hopefully) in the form of letters, words, sentences, and pictures. Hopefully, you're ignoring the sounds in the background, the sound of your own breath, or the feel of the clothes against your skin. You're making choices about blocking some stimuli while

Figure 3.1   Standard Memory Model or Information Processing Model

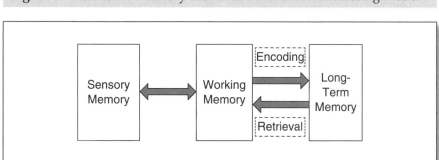

allowing others to move into your consciousness. If you didn't make these choices, creating meaning with this text would be very difficult.

Sense memory, sometimes called sensory register, is where this original sense data are registered. It has an unlimited capacity; however, it has a very short duration. It retains an exact copy of what is perceived, but this only lasts for one to three seconds.

Short-Term Memory

While the terms *short-term memory* and *working memory* are often used synonymously, technically they're different. Short-term memory (STM) is like a small holding pen for perceived data from sense memory. Short-term memory has a limited capacity. Most people can hold seven bits of information; however, some can hold up to nine bits and some only five bits. That's not a lot of information. Working memory (described below) is the space within short-term memory where you actually process or do something with the data that's there.

Holding More Bits

Chunking enables you to hold more information in STM. Chunking is the process of organizing bits of data into meaningful larger wholes in order to make more efficient use of the limited space in STM.

> **Experiment.** Find three people who are willing to be your lab rats for this experiment. Show rat number 1 the first list of digits in Figure 3.2 for 10 seconds and ask him or her to remember and repeat back as many as possible. Show rat number 2 the second list and ask him or her to do the same. Show rat number 3 the third list and ask him or her to do the same. You can see where we are going with this. You can hold a lot more stuff in STM if it is organized into meaningful groups.

Figure 3.2   Chunking

1 – 9 – 7 – 2 – 2 – 0 – 1 – 0 – 1 – 9 – 9 – 8 – 1 – 9 – 9 – 7

19 – 72 – 20 – 10 – 19 – 98 – 19 – 97

1972 – 2010 – 1998 – 1997

As an example, in my writing I tend to use a lot of analogies and metaphors. This is also a form of chunking. It's much easier to hold an image or concept in STM or to encode and retrieve it from LTM than a series of individual facts. Thus, connecting new facts or concepts to known images or concepts via analogy or metaphor makes it much easier to understand and remember them.

Learning to Read

The idea of chunking also applies to reading instruction. If instruction leads students to focus on individual letters, comprehension becomes more difficult. This is because students are only able to hold seven letters in STM as they're trying to create meaning with text. This happens when letter-by-letter phonics instruction is over-emphasized. If instead, reading instruction asks students to use minimal letter cues and rely also on semantic and syntactical cues, comprehension becomes much easier because there is more room in STM to focus on ideas. Students can hold seven letters or seven ideas in STM. Which do you think might be the most efficient and effective in terms of creating meaning with text?

To illustrate, I would again have you focus the reading process you are using right now. As you encounter the words on these pages, I would posit that you are not attending to each individual letter. You're using minimal letter cues and instead relying on context clues, sight words, phonograms, word parts, sentence syntax, and in many cases skipping words entirely. This is what real readers do when they create meaning with text. They don't read letter by letter.

Working Memory

Working memory is the workbench where information is held in STM as you do something with it. Whereas STM is a passive receptacle, working memory is an active space within STM used to work with information. What types of things might you do on this cognitive workbench? You could add to data, analyze data, organize data, restructure data, or make connections. Right now as you're reading about reading, you're searching through the files folders in your head (schemata) and pulling up what you know about this subject, including your own experiences reading and learning to read. You're connecting that old knowledge with the new information found on the page. Based on this old knowledge and your own reasoning process,

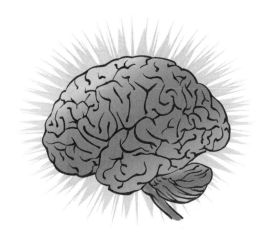

you're analyzing, evaluating, and deciding which information is interesting and useful, which is irrelevant, and which is totally kooky. When you find some interesting or important ideas the little person in your head will put these in the right file folder and put that folder in a place in your cognitive file cabinet where you can find it when it's again needed.

Working memory is also the place where *metacognition* takes place. *Meta* is a Greek word meaning to transcend or to go beyond, above, or higher. *Cognition* means thinking. Metacognition is to go beyond merely thinking and to think about thinking or monitor one's thought process. Metacognition in the act of reading means to monitor your comprehension. You're asking such questions as the following: "Do I understand what I am reading? Does this make sense? What's the important idea? Do I agree with this? Do I need to read this paragraph again? What is the main point in this chapter? How is this like something else I have learned?" Metacognition then involves thinking about thinking, checking for understanding, or monitoring your own thoughts. Through explicit instruction, we can improve students' metacognitive skills (see Chapters 13 and 14).

Automaticity

Automaticity is the act of performing a procedure or operation without thinking about it or with very little conscious awareness. This occurs when the steps or processes involved with a particular skill become automatic. For example, as we drive, most of us don't have to consciously think about pressing the gas pedal or break pedal or turning the wheel. We respond to the curves and stop signs we encounter automatically with very little conscious attention. If we had to devote a lot of our attention to each of these functions, we'd have less attention to devote to driving conditions, and we'd be far more likely to drive into something.

Likewise, when I play my guitar, I do not have to consciously think about each individual finger movement with the right hand strumming pattern or the left hand cord placement. The strumming patterns and finger positions have become automatic, enabling me to concentrate on other dimensions of the music. If I had to consciously attend to each finger placement I would be playing at a very rudimentary level for a long time.

Automaticity in reading usually refers to word recognition skills. Recognizing words automatically enables students to devote more space in STM to comprehending what they're reading. Chapters 10 and 11 contain a variety of strategies that can be used to help students identify words automatically as they read. And just like learning to drive a car, automaticity comes with practice. Hence, an effective, research-based strategy is to simply have students practice reading every day (Allington, 2012).

Long-Term Memory

Long-term memory (LTM) has an almost unlimited capacity to store information for an almost unlimited duration. This means that everything you've ever experienced is tucked away in a file cabinet in your mind somewhere. But if this is true, why is it that you can't remember certain things? Why do I forget to take out the garbage on Wednesday nights? And why did you get so many wrong on your ninth-grade history test? It's not a matter of storage; rather, of retrieval. That is, the information is still in our memory; we just have a hard time getting access to some of it.

During the process of reading, organized bits of knowledge stored in LTM called schemata are used to recognize words, make inferences and predictions, and to help you understand what you are reading (Paulson & Goodman, 2008). This is described in more detail below (see *schema theory*).

THE TWO-WAY FLOW OF INFORMATION

Notice in Figure 3.1 that the arrows point both to and from LTM in the information processing model. This reflects the two-way flow of information. In Chapter 1 this was described from a neurological perspective. This concept will be elaborated here from a cognitive perspective.

LTM to STM

We use the knowledge stored in our LTM to help make sense of the data in STM (Sternberg, 2009). The more knowledge we have about a particular topic, the easier it is to understand, process, and *encode* new related data. (Encode means to store information in LTM.) For example, I can read books related to literacy pretty easily with fairly high rates of comprehension, not because I'm so smart, but because the file cabinet in my head contains files that are jammed full of literacy information. This provides a rich context for understanding and predicting (Schraw, 2006). When I encounter a text related to literacy, the little man in my head knows exactly what to look for, where to store new information, and how it relates to other files in LTM.

But when I encounter information in a text about something that I know little about (such as financial planning), encoding is slow, inefficient, and labored. There are many more fixations and regressions with my eyeballs. I am able to understand and remember very little. This is because there are no related file folders in my head to help me make sense of this data. The little man in my head doesn't know how this new information connects to other things. He has to create new file folders and try to make connections as he analyzes this new information. The same brain is encountering both texts; the only difference is what is in that brain.

> **Experiment.** Go to a library and find a book on a subject you know quite a bit about and another book on a subject that you know little about. Look for books written at approximately the same reading level. Count off 200 words. Read each out loud as quickly as you can and have a friend time you. How did your times compare? Then pick one page at random from each book and read silently. After each page, list as many things as you can remember. What do you discover?

LTM to Perception

Knowledge in LTM also enhances our ability to perceive things as well (Goldstein, 2008). During the process of reading, this knowledge helps us to perceive important content words (Zeelenberg, Pecher, Shiffrin, & Raaijmakers, 2003). For example, when I read about literacy topics, I am able to perceive content-related words microseconds faster than the content-related words from unfamiliar topics. Again, it is the knowledge in LTM that enhances my ability to perceive content-related words on the page.

Schema Theory and Reading

Schema theory aptly accounts for the interactive processes described above. A *schema* (plural is schemata) is an organized body of knowledge stored in LTM related to specific concepts and experiences (like a file folder in your head). We use schemata to help us understand what we're experiencing, to learn and remember efficiently, and to make predictions related to what we're about to experience (Anderson, 2013; Schraw, 2006). For example, if you are about to enter a restaurant, your brain has already made predictions as to what this restaurant will look like based on all the restaurant

Source: Courtesy of www.clipart.com.

experiences you've had in your life. Your restaurant schema enables you to quickly assess the situation and to know what to do. Do you need to wait to be seated? Do you go someplace to order food? Is there a menu? Where and when do you pay? Think how complex this would be if you had never experienced a restaurant before.

In the same way, when we read, we use schemata to help us create meaning with text. Schemata are used to make predictions, fill in missing information, and to make inferences (Hruby & Goswami, 2013; Schraw, 2006; Strauss, 2011; Wagner & Stanovich, 1996; Weaver, 2009). Activating relevant schemata is also related to enhanced fluency, word identification, and comprehension (Anderson, 2013; McVee, Dunsmore, & Gauelek, 2013). In other words, we use what's in our head (schemata along with syntactic and semantic cueing) to help us make sense of what's on the page. This is the essence of the neurocognitive model of reading described in Chapter 1.

Last Word

This chapter described cognitive learning theory, the information processing model, and some of the ramifications for reading and reading instruction. I'll end with one related teaching tip: Find interesting and familiar things for your students to read. This enables them to use their schemata to help them create meaning with print. Of course the most interesting and familiar stories are those that students write themselves. Chapter 12 provides some strategies for helping students to create their own reading material.

Section II

Diagnosing Reading Problems, Documenting Progress, and Planning Instruction

4

Diagnosis and Documentation

A pig doesn't get any heavier by weighing it. A house doesn't get any warmer by adding thermostats. A standardized text by itself does nothing to improve the quality of education our children receive.

To be of value, assessment should inform instruction. That is, it should give you a sense of what to teach and how to teach. This is not the case with many standardized tests. They're often not very useful in planning for the instruction of individual students (Allington, 1994; Rasinski, Padak, & Fawecett, 2010). That is, they do little to inform teaching, especially for struggling readers and writers. This chapter focuses on one form of assessment that can inform reading instruction: the Diagnostic Reading Inventory.

DIAGNOSING THE PROBLEM

Here's the problem: You've got a student named Pat who's struggling to learn to read. His Individualized Education Program (IEP) tells you that Pat can't read very well. On his IEP you see a bunch of numbers from standardized tests. These numbers show you how much Pat can't read in comparison to everybody else. Percentages and percentile rankings are used to describe Pat in terms of his distance from average. But then what? At the end of the day Pat still can't read. You still don't know why Pat can't read and what specifically you should do about it.

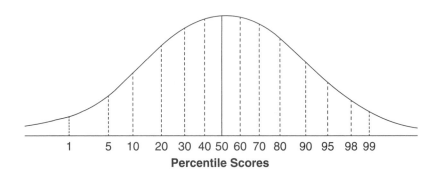

Percentile Scores

Limitations of Standardized Tests

There's nothing inherently wrong with standardized tests. They're one of many types of tools that can be useful in helping struggling readers; however, with any tool, you must recognize the limitations. For reading, I find that most standardized tests are insufficient for diagnosing the possible cause of a reading disability, identifying student strengths as well as specific areas for remediation, and providing information for planning and instruction. To do this, you need another type of tool. I recommend some form of a Diagnostic Reading Inventory (DRI).

Diagnostic Reading Inventory

A common term for a DRI is an Informal Reading Inventory (IRI). However, the term *Informal Reading Inventory* may imply to some that it's haphazard or that it's somehow less valuable than other "formal" types of measures. This isn't the case. In the hands of a knowledgeable teacher, a DRI provides valuable data than cannot be obtained on standardized tests (Allington, 1994). Thus, I prefer the term *Diagnostic Reading Inventory*. With the DRI, the examiner is not simply following a formula and list of sequential steps. Instead, the knowledge and experience of the experienced teacher becomes an integral part of the assessment (Weaver, 2009).

Figure 4.1 contains a list of common, commercially prepared DRIs. The information in this chapter will enable you to use any of these. This chapter will also enable you to design and implement your own DRI.

Figure 4.1   Common Diagnostic Reading Inventories

- *Qualitative Reading Inventory*, 5th edition (Leslie and Caldwell)
- *Reading Inventory for the Classroom*, 5th edition (Flynt and Cooter)
- *Classroom Reading Inventory*, 12th edition (Silvaroli and Wheelock)
- *Basic Reading Inventory*, 10th edition (Johns)
- *Analytical Reading Inventory*, 9th edition (Woods and Moe)
- *Ekwall/Shanker Reading Inventory*, 6th edition (Shanker and Ekwall)
- *Informal Reading Inventory*, 8th edition (Roe and Burns)

A DRI can be used to determine students' approximate independent and instructional reading levels (see Figure 4.2), as well as their strength and deficit areas related to word identification, fluency, and/or comprehension. The basic elements include graded word lists, graded reading passages, and comprehension questions or a maze. Each of these is described below.

Figure 4.2   Independent, Instructional, and Frustration Levels

- **Independent Level.** At this level students can read unassisted. They are generally able to identify 98% or more of the words. Comprehension scores are 90% or higher. When students read independently for pleasure, you want them to be reading at this level or BELOW.
- **Instructional Level.** At this level, students can read with some assistance. They are generally able to identify 90–97% of these words. Comprehension scores are between 75% and 89%. This is the level of reading material that should be used for reading instruction. Here you will need to provide some assistance such as a story map, vocabulary help, scaffolded oral reading, or a story preview.
- **Frustration Level.** At this level students cannot be successful even with a lot of the teacher's help. They are able to identify 89% or less of these words. Comprehension scores are less than 75%. Avoid any type of reading at this level. Challenging students with frustration level material will NOT help them progress faster. Reading at this level results only in frustrated students who learn that they can't learn to read and that they don't like reading.

GRADED WORD LISTS

Graded word lists provide a very general estimation of students' reading grade level. These are used to inform the next part of the DRI. An example of a graded word list can be found in Figure 4.3. A variety of public-use, graded word lists can be found on the Internet.

Figure 4.3   Example of a Graded Word List

Directions: Start with a list you believe to be two levels below the student's current reading grade level. Have the student read each word out loud. Continue until the student makes three or more errors.

Reading Levels: 1 error = independent level; 2 errors = instruction level; 3 or more errors = frustration level

Independent _____ Instructional _____ Frustration _____

Primer	First Grade	Second Grade	Third Grade	Fourth Grade
was	please	beautiful	magic	predict
could	flower	everyone	beginning	knowledge
children	man	should	thankful	canoe
know	brown	write	crawl	vicious
what	children	sorry	museum	decorate
saw	father	people	reason	windshield
around	drop	instead	bush	parachute
mother	birthday	breakfast	planet	official
now	men	cupcake	discover	dignity
old	kind	eyes	enough	island

These are the steps for using graded word lists:

1. Start two or more levels below students' estimated reading grade level.

2. Ask the student to read the word list out loud. Have a duplicate list in front of you to keep track of the words correctly identified. Circle the words that aren't correctly identified.

3. Go to the next list. Keep moving up until you reach the student's frustration level (see Figure 4.3).

4. Based on the information from these word lists, select a graded reading passage that is at the student's independent reading level for the next part of the DRI.

GRADED READING PASSAGES

Graded reading passages are texts that have been normed for a particular grade level. This means that the average student at a particular grade level could read the passage independently. For example, reading level 3 (RL 3) means that 50% or more of all third-grade students could read that passage at the independent level. Sometimes graded readers are broken down further by month. RL 3.2 means the student is reading at the third grade, second month. The commercially prepared DRIs listed in Figure 4.1 have graded reading passages included. However, you can prepare your own DRI by using basal readers that have been normed for a particular level or children's books. On the back of most children's books you will see RL followed by a number. This indicates the approximate reading grade level.

These are the steps for using the graded reading passages:

1. Record each session with an audio recorder. You will need to go back later to carefully analyze students' reading.

2. Give the student a copy of a graded passage that is at his or her independent reading level based on the graded word lists above. Provide the title of the passage and then ask the student to read it out loud. Tell the student that some of the words may be unknown. Provide help or hints only when absolutely necessary. Give the student plenty of space to self-correct words and sentences but use your teacher sense to avoid frustration. Remember, the purpose here is to collect data. Frustrating students will affect the quantity and quality of the data you get.

3. You should have a copy of what the student is reading in front of you. As the student reads, put a line through each miscued words. A miscue is when what the student says does not match what is on the page (see Figure 4.7 on page 46). Also, make quick notes of some of your initial impressions in the margins as the student is reading. Focus on things such as facial expression, body language, general confidence, and word identification strategies used. Note anything that stands out here. This is all important data that will help you understand each reader.

Figure 4.4   Example of a Scoring Guide for Comprehension Questions

Comprehension	
# Correct	**Level**
5½ to 6	Independent
4½ to 5	Instructional
4 or less	Frustration

But do not try to write too much here. You will be going back later to listen to the audio recording in order to engage in a more thorough and precise analysis.

4. Most commercially prepared DRIs have five or six comprehension questions followed by a scoring guide (Figure 4.4). After reading the passage orally, ask these questions and record students' responses. Note that the comprehension part of the DRI is optional. If you are creating your own DRI and you want to assess comprehension, use some form of a story retelling rubric (see Figure 4.10 on page 51).

5. If the student is able to identify 98% of the words or more (independent reading level), move up to the next reading level passage. Commercially prepared DRIs will indicate exactly what this number is. If you are using your own graded reading passage, count the number of words and figure out percentages before administering the DRI. Stop when the student reaches his or her instructional level (90% to 97% of words correctly identified). We can assume that text above the student's instructional level is the frustration level. For example, if a student's instructional level is at Grade 2, we can assume that third-grade reading passages and above will be at this student's frustration level.

There may be differences in word identification and comprehension levels. For example, when reading a passage at the second-grade level Pat might correctly identify 98% of the words (independent level), yet score only 75% on comprehension measures (instructional level). This tells us that comprehension, not word identification, is an area to focus on.

Qualitative Data Analysis

It usually works best to do the initial qualitative data analysis as soon as you have finished working with a student. In this way, the experience is fresh in your memory. In the qualitative data analysis, you focus on observed behaviors related to fluency and word identification, the student's general demeanor, and your overall impressions.

These are the steps for conducting a qualitative data analysis:

1. Before listening to your audio recordings, do a quick analysis. Write directly on the copy of the graded reading passage you used above. Was the student able to read the passage fairly easily and create meaning? Or did the student struggle? What type of reading behaviors did you notice? What was your impression of that student's attempt to create meaning with print? Describe any interesting or important analyses, descriptions, or observations.

2. Analyze the word identification strategies used while reading. The questions in Figure 4.5 can be used to inform your analysis.

3. Analyze students' reading fluency. The questions in Figure 4.6 can be used to inform your analysis.

Figure 4.5   Listening for Word Identification Strategies

1. What does the student do to identify words?

2. Does the student use context clues?

3. Does the student recognize word parts?

4. Does the student use onsets to identify unknown words?

5. Does the student overuse phonics?

6. Does the student self-correct?

7. Are the miscues schema-related?

8. What types of miscues does the student make?

9. Does the student recognize and use morphemes (prefixes, suffixes, and roots)?

10. Does the student correctly identify the onset or beginnings of miscued words?

Figure 4.6 Listening for Reading Fluency

1. Is the reading choppy, word-by-word?
2. Is the reading choppy, letter-by-letter?
3. Does the student pause at the ends of sentences (prosody)?
4. Is the inflection appropriate to the sentence or passage?
5. Does the student pause to check for understanding (metacognition)?

Miscue Analysis

Now you are ready to conduct the miscue analysis portion of the DRI. A *reading miscue* is anytime there is a difference between what is on the page and what students say. We do not use the word "error" because reading miscues often represent mature reading behavior. Four types of miscues and their meanings are described in Figure 4.7.

Figure 4.7 Hierarchy of Miscues

Types of Miscues

- **Meaningful Miscue.** Sentences still retain the original meaning
- **Schema-Related Miscue.** Similar concept, sentence meaning not retained
- **Significant Miscue.** Sentence meaning not retained
- **Meaningless Pronunciation.** Correctly sounding out words without meaning

Each type of miscue tells you something different about how individual students are creating meaning with print.

- A *meaningful miscue* is one that does not change the fundamental meaning of the sentence. For example: If the student said, "The dogs run down the road," instead of "The dogs ran down the road," this would not change the meaning of the sentences. I recommend that this be counted as half a miscue. Write a large "M" with a circle around it to indicate that it was a meaningful miscue.

- A second type of miscue that is of interest, but not necessarily something you need to document, is the *schema-related miscue*. A *schema* is an organized knowledge structure in long-term memory. Schemata (plural of schema) are essential for understanding the world around us as well as learning and comprehending. If a miscue fundamentally changes the meaning of the sentence but is still very much related to the passage, write a large "S" above it with a circle around it to indicate that it is schema-related. It is still counted as a miscue; however, this tells us that the student is engaged in a meaningful reading behavior: using background knowledge. An example of a schema-related miscue includes the following: In reading a passage about making roads the students said, "The truck made the road smooth" instead of "The grader made the road smooth." This is a significant miscue as it changes the meaning of the sentence. A truck is much different than a grader. However, trucks and graders are both used in the making of the road.

- *A significant miscue* is what we most commonly think of as a mistake. Here the miscue changes the meaning of the sentence or does not make sense within the sentence, the students skips the word, or the student needs help with the word. If the sentence was, "The dogs ran down the road," and students said, "The dogs rammed down the road," or "The dogs rode down the road," these would be significant miscues as they fundamentally changed the meaning of the sentence.

- There is a fourth type of miscue that is not technically a miscue and should not be counted as such. A *meaningless pronunciation* is when students correctly sound out the word, but it is clear that they have no understanding of the word. You can tell by their inflection if they understand the word. It is often pronounced in the form of a question. "Fossils?" Or, the individual parts of the word may be pronounced correctly, but they are put together in a stilted or imprecise way. This involves some judgment on your part; however, the power of the DRI is that it provides a structure for you to use your experience and teacher insight to understand students as meaning makers. If you wish to document this, put an "MP" with a circle around it just above the word.

  The meaningless pronunciation tells you something about students' conceptual and word knowledge. There are three possible reasons for a meaningless pronunciation: (a) students do not have a concept to match the word in long-term memory, (b) students conception of the word does not match the context that the word was found in, or (c) students were not able to make the link between the word and the concept. This information can be used to design future lessons for both vocabulary and concept lessons.

These are the steps for conducting a miscue analysis:

1. Go back and listen to the audio recording of the graded passages. Put a line through the miscued words and write down exactly what the student said above the word (see Figure 4.8). If

the student made a miscue but went back and corrected it, it is not counted as a miscue. This is a self-correction. Self-correcting is a mature reading behavior. This means that the student is monitoring his or her comprehension (metacognition). On your scoring sheet write "SC" with a circle around it on top of the word. SCs are good.

Figure 4.8   Miscue Analysis

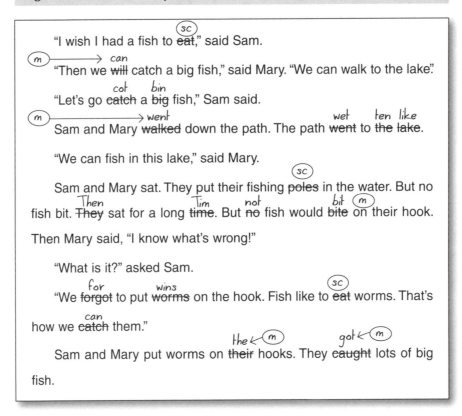

2. Using the DRI analysis sheet in Figure 4.9, write the target word in the first column and what students actually said in the second column. Indicate with a tally mark whether it was a meaningful miscue in the next columns.

3. Significant miscues count as one miscue; meaningful miscues count as half a miscue. Do not count proper names as a miscue. If students skip an entire line, count this as one miscue. Add up the total number of miscues.

4. Under the "Analysis" section, record the total number of self-corrections. If a story retelling rubric (see Figure 4.10) or

Figure 4.9   DRI Analysis Sheet

DRI Analysis Sheet

Student:_____ Date:_____

Reading level of graded reading passage: _____

Target Word	Miscue	Meaningful Miscue	
		Yes	No
*Totals _____			
Total Miscues: _____			

Analysis

# Self-Corrections	Fluency WPM	Comprehension
		_____ %
		ind — instr — frust

Miscues

# Total Miscues	# Not Miscued	# Total Words	Percentage
			_____ %

Patterns or types of miscues (use the back):

*Some reading experts count meaningful miscues as only half a miscue; others do not count them at all. I recommend counting them as half a miscue.

comprehension questions were used, record the percentage correctly answered, and indicate whether it was at the independent, instructional, or frustration level.

5. Determine the reading rate or average words-per-minute (WPM). To do this, record the time it took for students to complete the passage. Divide the time (in seconds) by 60. For example, if you read a passage in 90 seconds, you would divide 90 by 60: $90 \div 60 = 1.5$ minutes. Divide this (1.5) by the total number of words. If the total number of words is 119, then you read 119 words in 1.5 minutes: $119 \div 1.5 = 79$ WPM.

6. Under the "Miscues" section of the DRI analysis sheet record the total number of miscues. Subtract the number of miscued words from the total number of words to get the number of nonmiscued words. To figure out the percentage of words correctly identified, divide the nonmiscued words by the total number of words and multiply by 100. Use this percentage to indicate general reading levels (98% or better = independent; 90%–97% = instructional; 89% or less = frustration); however, recognize that this only represents word identification (it does not include comprehension).

7. Review the first two columns of the DRI analysis sheet. Look for patterns in the types of miscues students made. Was there a pattern related to beginning, middle, or ending sounds? Vowel sounds? Did certain phonograms give the student trouble? Were they able to identify the beginning sound but not the blend? This will inform the type of instruction needed for word identification.

ASSESSING COMPREHENSION

In assessing students' ability to comprehend, keep in mind that students' ability to read any text is influenced by their familiarity with the topic and the words used, whether it is narrative or expository text, the style of writing, and the construction of the sentences. Described here are two simple ways to assess comprehension. These can be used if you are creating your own DRI.

Story Retelling

Story retelling is a simple way to get a sense of students' ability to comprehend narrative text. For this, use a graded reading passage or story that is at students' independent level. Identify the important characters, settings, and events in the story and write them in a Story Retelling Chart, similar to Figure 4.10, before the assessment. After reading the story, ask students to retell the story. As they name each of the items in the Story Retelling Chart, give them one point. If, after retelling the story, they have not named all, ask them directly. Example: "Can you name any other characters in this story? Can you name any other places where this story took place?" Give students one point for correct responses here. If they still cannot name one of the elements, provide a simple hint. These are prompted and worth half a point. Thus far, your Story Retelling Chart contains only low-level story details. You can include one or two inference questions. These are questions related to something implied but not specifically stated in the story. Inference questions should be worth two points.

Figure 4.10   Story Retelling Chart

Story Retelling Chart

Name: _____ Grade: _____ Date: _____

Story Title: _____ Reading Level: _____

	Unprompted	Prompted
CHARACTERS: 1 point each		
1.		
2.		
3.		
4.		
5.		
SETTING: 1 point each		
1.		
2.		
3.		
EVENTS: 1 point each		
1.		
2.		
3.		

(Continued)

(Continued)

INFERENCE QUESTIONS: 2 points each		
1.		
2.		
TOTAL POINTS: ___/100 = ___%	___/100	___/100

Unprompted = 1 point
Prompted = ½ point

Independent reading level = 90%–100% accuracy
Instruction level = 75%–89% accuracy
Frustration level = 74% or lower

Maze

A *maze* can also be used to assess comprehension of narrative or expository text (see Figure 4.11). To create these, use a graded reading passage of approximately 125 to 150 words. After the first sentence, delete every fifth word. Provide three alternatives from which to choose. The choices should include the following: the correct response, an incorrect response that has the same grammatical function as the deleted word, and an incorrect response with a different grammatical function. There should be a total of 20 deleted words.

Figure 4.11   Example of a Maze

Prairie Dogs

Prairie dogs are small, burrowing rodents. They live in short-grass [**prairies** – oceans – big] and the high plains [**of** – in – said] the western USA and Mexico. [**They** – her – up] will eat all sorts [**of** – it – many] vegetables and fruits.

Independent level = 85% or above
Instructional level = 50% to 84%
Frustration level = 49% or less

PUTTING IT TOGETHER

At this point the data should give you a sense of the student's independent and instructional reading levels. This enables you to use the appropriate level of reading material for instruction and help students select appropriate books for independent reading. You should also have some diagnostic data to indicate if the student is struggling with fluency, word identification, comprehension, or combinations of these. And finally, you should know what kinds of strategies the student is using to identify words.

Three Deficit Areas

Readers struggle because of deficits in one or more of the three areas examined by the DRI: fluency, word identification, and comprehension (Caldwell & Leslie, 2013).

Fluency

Fluency is the ability to process text quickly and efficiently (see Chapter 12). Figure 4.12 contains a list of very approximate fluency norms for oral reading rates. The WPM scores you get provide a very general sense of where the individual student is at in comparison to other students at the same grade level; however, your qualitative analysis above will provide a better sense of the student's ability to read fluently than will a simple number.

Figure 4.12   Very Approximate "Norms" for Oral Reading Rates

At the end of that grade, students should be able to read material at their grade level at the approximate levels below:

1st grade: 53 WPM
2nd grade: 89 WPM
3rd grade: 107 WPM
4th grade: 123 WPM
5th grade: 139 WPM
6th grade: 150 WPM
7th grade: 150 WPM
8th grade: 151 WPM

Word Identification

Word Identification skills are what students use to identify unknown words as they are reading. As described in Chapter 11, there are six general types of word identification skills that students use when a word is not recognized automatically: (a) analogy [word parts or word families], (b) morphemic analysis [prefixes, suffixes, and roots], (c) semantics [context clues], (d) syntax [grammar and word order], (e) sight words, and (f) phonics. The qualitative analysis will enable you to determine the way the student identifies unknown words, this student's strengths and deficits, and the types of miscues this student tends to make.

Comprehension

Comprehension is the ability to create meaning with text. With struggling readers, it is sometimes difficult to know if or to what extent deficits in the areas of fluency and word identification affect comprehension. However, the DRI enables you to separate word identification and fluency issues from comprehension. If you want to focus on listening comprehension, read the graded reading passage to students and use the Story Retelling Chart to assess.

Planning for Instruction

In the chapters that follow, you will be given specific strategies to develop students' abilities in the three areas above as well as other areas. There are three recommendations:

First, it is imperative that students not be frustrated or overwhelmed. Chapter 8 describes the negative impact that these emotions can have on students' learning. For any intervention or short-term plan, set short, attainable goals (books read or pages read), and make a big deal out of making goals. Instruction should be proximal or just a little ahead of students' independent level.

Second, struggling readers often have difficulties with phonics. It may seem counter-intuitive, but instead of focusing exclusively on what students can't do as they read, focus on what they can do. That is, plan instructional activities to develop their other two-cueing systems (semantics and syntax) as well as phonics. Focusing only on letter-sound associations will make reading more abstract and less enjoyable. Also, failure increases stress and reduces learning. You can still include word work that develops the phonological cueing system, but do not let the other two-cueing systems atrophy.

Finally, use a comprehensive approach to reading instruction that includes all the essential elements described in Chapter 6: All these elements do NOT need to be included in each lesson. This would be very hard to do. But in your curriculum and over the course of a week, all elements should be addressed to varying degrees.

Reliability, Validity, Intervention Plans, and IEPs

Finally, with any type of educational test or measure, issues of reliability and validity must be addressed. Reliability in statistical terms refers to repeatability or consistency. With assessment, it refers to how often and to what degree you get the same scores or results on a particular measure. For example, if a student scores 98% on the measure one day and 62% on the measure another day, we would need to consider the reliability of the measure (or the reliability of the student).

Validity refers to the extent that the test or assessment device measures what it says it is measuring. For example, the language arts portion of an achievement test usually assesses discrete grammar and punctuation skills. It would not be a very valid assessment of students' ability to write, just as measures of how many pushups you could do or how fast you could run would not be a very valid assessment of one's ability to play tennis.

In educational assessments, there is often a trade-off between reliability and validity. With a DRI, there is some subjectivity built into the measure. That is, it is going to differ slightly from teacher to teacher, and this is as it should be. But in the hands of a knowledgeable teacher, the DRI will always give you an accurate and reliable portrait of individual students as readers. It also provides data that will enable you to identify useful goals and benchmarks for intervention plans and IEPs that are directly related to students' specific deficit areas. Figure 4.13 shows an example of such goals and benchmarks. For intervention plans and IEPs, I strongly recommend that you have specific goals and benchmarks for each of the three deficit areas that are relevant.

Figure 4.13 Goals and Benchmarks for Intervention Plans and IEPs

---

GOAL 1—Fluency

Pat will read 100 WPM at reading level 4 (RL 4).

Benchmark

1. Pat will read 100 WPM at RL 3.
2. Pat will read 60 WPM at RL 4.
3. Pat will read 80 WPM at RL 4.

Measuring Progress

Progress will be measured using timed readings with graded readers.

GOAL 2—Word Identification

On a graded reader with at least 200 words, Pat will correctly identify 90% of the words—RL 4.

Benchmark

1. Pat will correctly identify 90% of the words on a graded reader—RL 3.
2. Pat will correctly identify 50% of the words on a graded reader—RL 4.
3. Pat will correctly identify 70% of the words on a graded reader—RL 4.

Measuring Progress

Progress will be measured using running records on graded readers.

GOAL 3—Comprehension: Narrative Text

On a graded reader (RL 4) using narrative text, Pat will identify major characters, events, and settings with at least 90% success.

Benchmark

1. On a graded reader (RL 3) using narrative text, Pat will identify major characters, events, and settings with at least 70% success.
2. On a graded reader (RL 3) using narrative text, Pat will identify major characters, events, and settings with at least 90% success.
3. On a graded reader (RL 4) using narrative text, Pat will identify major characters, events, and settings with at least 70% success.

Measuring Progress

Scores will be measured using a story retelling rubric.

Last Word

This chapter described the Diagnostic Reading Inventory. I've simplified the processes used here related to miscue analysis. After reading this chapter, you should be able to use any of the commercial products listed in Figure 4.1. You should also be able to design your own DRI. I've used variations of a DRI for several years. From my perspective, it would be very hard to set usable IEP goals or to adequately design any type of intervention or instructional plan without this type of diagnostic instrument.

5

Reading Lessons

We don't really teach reading; rather, we create the conditions whereby students can develop their ability to create meaning with print.

This chapter describes three types of reading lessons: (a) SRE lessons, (b) guided reading lessons, and (c) shared reading lessons. Each of these can be used in some way when working with struggling readers.

SRE LESSON

The *scaffolded reading experience* (SRE) lesson is a type of reading lesson that enables students to read a text independently (Johnson & Graves, 1997). Each part of this is described below (see Figure 5.1).

Lesson Purpose Statement

The purpose statement provides focus for the rest of your lesson. The purpose of your SRE lesson is either to help students read and enjoy a story (narrative text) or to read and understand informational

Figure 5.1   SRE Reading Lesson Format

SRE Reading Lesson Format

I.   **Lesson Purpose Statement.** This element describes the reason for the lesson.

    1.   **Narrative Text.** Students will read and enjoy [insert story or chapter title here].

    2.   **Expository Text.** Students will read and understand [insert book or chapter title here].

II. **Pre-Reading Activity:** The pre-reading activity gets students ready to read the story.

Always make a link or bridge from the pre-reading activity to the story or text.

III. **During Reading.** This element describes how students will read the assigned reading selection.

IV. **Post-Reading Activity.** The post-reading activity should be an activity designed to get students to manipulate or become engaged with an idea from the story.

books, articles, or chapters (expository text). Thus, your purpose statement would look like one of the following:

> **Narrative Text.** Students will read and enjoy [insert story or chapter title here].

> **Expository Text.** Students will read and understand [insert book, article, or chapter title here].

In your SRE lesson, everything that follows should support your purpose statement. Reading independently should not be confused with learning a reading subskill. Confusing these two aspects of reading instruction will diminish the effectiveness of each. If there is something in your SRE lesson that does not support your purpose statement, take it out.

Pre-Reading Activity

The pre-reading activity should generally be two to five minutes in duration (with informational text, it is sometimes longer than this).

Here you want to provide the structure or scaffolding necessary to enable students to read the text independently. Keep this as short as possible while still providing the structure necessary for independent reading.

Below, nine pre-reading activities are described:

1. **Story Preview.** This is very much like a movie preview. Provide the basic essence of the story without revealing the ending. End with a catch of some sort. Example: "Read to find out what happens when . . . "

2. **Story Map.** A story map is any visual representation of the salient story elements. These can come in a variety of forms. I prefer maps that are basic and have just the story events listed using words or picture clues (see Figure 5.2). The story map provides the basic structure of the story. Preview each part of the story map before reading.

3. **Relevant Schemata.** A schema is a file folder in your head composed of related information (see Chapter 3). Before reading, help students recall what they know about a subject. This works best for expository text but can be used with narrative text on occasions. For example, before reading a chapter on amphibians you would ask students, "What do we know about amphibians?" As students tell you, list these on the board or chart.

4. **Background Information.** This works best for expository text. Use the headings of the text as an outline and teach the salient elements of what students are about to read. Their independent reading would then enable them to fill in the blanks. For students with severe reading difficulties, provide them with a partially completed outline before they read. Here you include headings and some salient elements underneath. Go over the outline with students before they read then ask them to fill in the missing parts as they read.

5. **Character Analysis.** A quick character analysis of the main characters would include those characteristics you believe are necessary to understand the story. These may be things such as the following: age, gender, story events, actions, and personal characteristics, traits, habits, and so forth. Make this as visual as possible using charts or pictures when feasible. A character analysis should always be printed on a board, poster, or interactive whiteboard for students to see and refer to.

6. **Story Grammar.** As a pre-reading strategy, story grammar works best if you keep it simple (see Chapter 13). Focus only on characters,

Figure 5.2   Examples of Story Maps

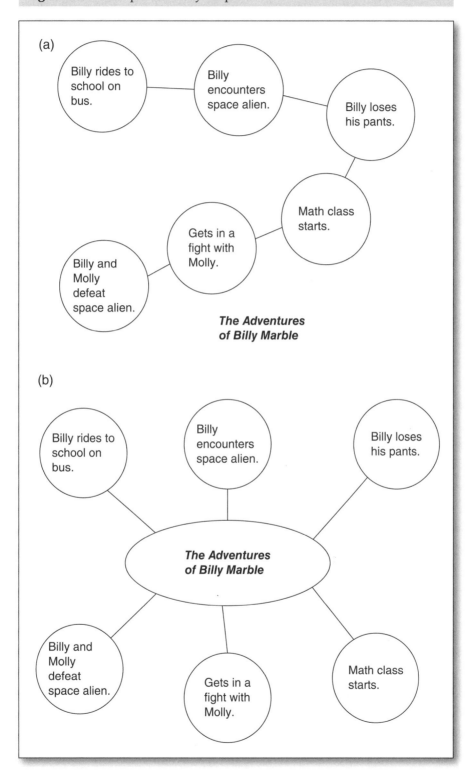

events, and settings. I recommend using the basic story grammar chart in Figure 5.3. Identify the salient elements here without giving away the story plot. If you wish to also use this as a during and post-reading activity, identify just some of the elements up front and ask students to identify the others as they are reading. This keeps them actively engaged as they read.

Figure 5.3   Basic Story Grammar Chart

Characters	Events	Settings
1.	1.	1.
2.	2.	2.
3.	3.	3.

7. **Important Vocabulary Words**. This pre-reading activity pertains mostly to expository text. Present three to five (no more than five) new or relatively unfamiliar words that are important to understanding the text. Always present words in the context of the sentence in which they are found, and display them so students can see them. Read them through with students and help them to generate at least two synonymous words or phrases (if possible). For more technical words and related contexts, present them in the context of a concept map or diagram.

8. **Advanced Organizers**. An advanced organizer is anything that shows the structure of what is to be read in advance of reading the text (see Figure 5.4). Concept maps and semantic maps work well with informational text (see Chapter 14). These can also be used to introduce new vocabulary words (see Chapter 15).

9. **Short Related Discussion.** Design a short discussion related to something found in the text. For example, if the character faces an ethical dilemma, create one or two related discussion questions. This takes a bit of creativity and planning if it is to be effective. In any kind of discussion, you should have two or three questions planned in advanced and written in your lesson plan. Use the action words in Bloom's taxonomy to help you design these (see Figure 5.7 on page 70). Strive to ask open-ended questions (questions for which you do not know the answers).

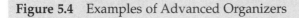

Figure 5.4   Examples of Advanced Organizers

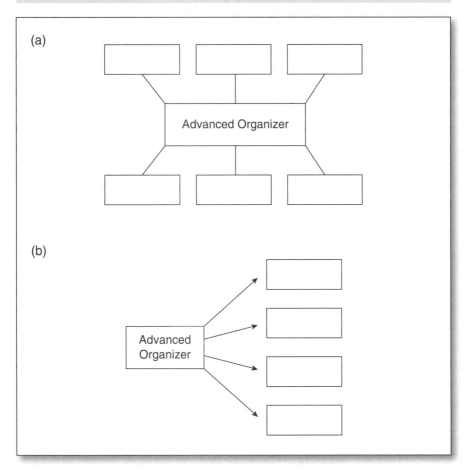

Two Important Points. Two things to remember before going to the next element: First, the goal of the pre-reading activity is to enable students to read the upcoming text independently. You want to provide as much or little structure as possible to enable them to do this. Second, always make a link or bridge from the pre-reading activity to the story or text.

During-Reading Activity

This element of the SRE lesson describes how students will read the assigned reading selection. You should very rarely (if ever) use round-robin reading or popcorn reading (see Chapter 12). This is where students go around the room or table with one person reading orally while the others follow along. We are preparing real people to interact in a real world. Round-robin reading is not how real people read in the real world. As well, this does nothing to help students learn to create meaning with text and serves to frustrate or embarrass students with reading difficulties. Below are some appropriate during-reading activities.

1. **Silent Reading**. This should be the most common option used in a SRE lesson. Here students read the selection silently. So how do you know if students are reading? You don't. But that's not the purpose here. There are plenty of places in your reading curriculum to measure and assess comprehension. This is not one of them. The goal of the SRE lesson is to enable students to read independently. They won't learn to do this if you do not provide opportunities for them to do so.

2. **Buddy Reading or Partner Reading.** Here students are paired with another student to read the selection orally. Have them find a place on the floor or around the room and read every other page, section, or paragraph. As they read, you are able to walk around the room and do a quick informal assessment. Some teachers use a clipboard and take anecdotal notes recording the types of miscues students make. These become the basis for the next minilesson used in a guided reading lesson (below).

3. **Whisper Reading.** This works best for younger students. Here each student reads using a quiet whisper voice.

4. **Shared Reading** (see description below).

Post-Reading Activity

The post-reading activity should be designed to get students to manipulate, extend, apply, analyze, or become engaged with an idea from the story or text. Avoid comprehension worksheets. These do very little, if anything, to help students comprehend. They also tend to make the experience less pleasurable. There are times and places to measure comprehension and to hold students accountable for information found in a text. The SRE lesson is not one of them. Look for open-ended activities that might include in of the activities described in later chapters of this book.

GUIDED READING LESSON

Terms and definitions vary in regards to guided reading and shared reading. The term "guided reading" in this book will be used to denote a small-group strategy for teaching specific skills, including word identification skills, comprehension skills, and thinking skills. The purpose is to provide direct and explicit instruction to small groups in an authentic reading context.

Planning a Guided Reading Lesson

The steps in planning a guided reading lesson are as follows:

1. **Identify students and specific instructional needs.** Guided reading groups should be small and flexible, composed of one to eight students of similar reading levels.

2. **Identify specific skills to teach or letters and letter patterns to reinforce.** Keep sessions focused and purposeful by identifying one or two skills to teach or letters and letter patterns to reinforce. Trying to teach too many skills in one guided reading session will diminish the impact of the lesson. Remember, students learn skills by being exposed to them over time in different ways and in different contexts.

3. **Identify suitable text at the approximate independent or instructional level.** If you are teaching comprehension skills, find text that is at students' instructional reading level. If you are teaching other kinds of skills, use text that is at students' independent reading level. A shorter text is preferable to a longer text (one to three paragraphs for primary age students; three to eight paragraphs for intermediate and older students). If you are using a longer book, use only part of the book for guided reading. Also, texts that students find interesting or amusing always make instruction easier and more effective.

4. **Decide on the type of reading material.** Guided reading lessons can be done using a big book; picture book; photocopied text; text on overhead, interactive whiteboard, or slide presentation; or text found on a website (if everyone has access to a computer). However, it is ideal for students have a physical copy of the text in front of them. In all cases, all students must be able to easily see and read the text.

5. **Create structure and design instruction**. Look for appropriate places within the text to stop for instruction and modeling of specific skills.

6. **Decide on the mode of reading.** The majority of time, students will read the text in one of three ways. They will follow along silently as the teacher reads aloud, read portions of the text silently to themselves, or whisper read (this allows you to listen in). With younger students it may be appropriate to use choral reading or echo reading (see Chapter 7). Choral reading is where the class reads the text together with you. Echo reading is where you read a line and students echo that same line back to you. As always, adopt and adapt to meet the needs of your students.

7. **Design a post-reading activity**. The purpose of guided reading is to teach a specific skill. The lesson becomes more effective if you include a short, simple independent activity at the end of the lesson that enables students to practice the skill learned during the lesson.

A Note About Guided Reading

Guided reading as defined here is a particular type of lesson plan structure used to teach skills. It should only be used to teach specific skills. In this sense, it is different from the SRE lesson plan described above where the purpose is to enable students to read a story or text independently. It is also different from the shared reading lesson described below where the purpose is to have a shared conversation around a text with students of varying reading levels.

SHARED READING LESSON

The term *shared reading* in this book will be used to denote a strategy that enables a multilevel class to share common discussions around a single book or text. Here students of varying ability levels interact with concepts, vocabulary, and ideas in authentic contexts in creative and engaging ways. (Note: Being a struggling reader or having a learning disability does not mean that these students have thinking disabilities. Students at all reading and learning levels need to have opportunities to participate in creative and engaging thinking activities.) And while shared reading is designed around a common text; *it is not, nor should it ever become, a venue for round robin reading.*

• **Primary Grades.** In the early primary grades shared reading is often done using a picture book with students sitting on a carpet. Here the teacher reads while students simply listen. It can also be done with a big book.

• **Intermediate Grades and Above.** In the intermediate grades and above, shared reading can be used with short sections of a novel, textbook, magazine article, newspaper article, or even a website. (Shared reading is a strategy that is very appropriate for middle school and high school.) All students need to be able to see and easily read the text. Text can be photocopied, put on an overhead projector or interactive whiteboard, or displayed using a slide presentation.

During-Reading Strategies

Students can follow along as you read the text or you can use one of the following strategies.

ERT

Reading a large amount of text may be overwhelming for some students in a mixed ability shared reading experience. The ERT silent reading strategy can be used with intermediate grades and above to alleviate this. ERT stands for everybody-read-to. Students are told to read to a particular point, usually one to four paragraphs at a time depending on the level. Examples:

"Everybody read to the second paragraph on page 13. I'll be asking you to identify one interesting or important idea. Look up when you have finished."

"Billy seems to be angry. I wonder what will happen next. Read to the bottom of page 7 to find out. Raise your thumb when you finish so that I know."

Students read silently to that spot and wait for your question or activity. Slower readers are usually able to get enough of the information to participate in the discussion even if they are not able to finish reading to the designated spot. What they aren't able to read, they will be able to assimilate through the discussion that takes place.

Every-Other

Related to ERT, read a paragraph or section out loud and have students read the next paragraph or section silently. Questions, conversations, or activities should always follow the silent reading.

Planning a Shared Reading Experience

The steps for planning a shared reading experience are as follows:

1. **Select and preview text to be read**. Initially, the piece of text chosen should be relatively short. As you and your students become more comfortable with this process, longer texts can be used. For older students, look for text that's related to a unit being studied or a book currently being read in a literacy class.

2. **Decide on the type of reading material.** Use one of the following: big book, picture book, or photocopied text; or put text on a slide presentation, interactive whiteboard, or some other projecting device.

3. **Decide on the mode of reading.** Use one of the modes of reading described above.

4. **Design a pre-reading activity**. Use any of the pre-reading strategies listed in Figure 5.5 to provide enough structure for students to read independently.

5. **Design questions and activities**. Look for appropriate places within the text to stop (use ERT or every other for older students). Design text-related questions or activities for use here. The questions in Figure 5.5 are designed for use with narrative text. The questions in Figure 5.6 are designed for use with expository text. We teach the process to develop the skill. This means that by doing these types of activities, students will eventually learn to ask these kinds of questions themselves as they are reading.

6. **Design a post-reading activity.** Design a post-reading activity that invites students to interact with, respond to, extend, apply, analyze, discuss, evaluate, or manipulate ideas or concepts found in the text. You can create post-reading activities based on any of the questions found in Figures 5.5 and 5.6 or use Bloom's taxonomy and action words in Figure 5.7.

Figure 5.5   Questions for Shared Reading: Narrative Text

To preview:

1. What do you think this story is about? What clues do you see in the title or cover of the book?

2. What does the title tell us?

3. What are some interesting things you see on the cover of the book?

4. What do you know about ___?

To check for understanding:

1. What is the story about?

2. What is the problem?

3. What do I want to know more about?

4. What do I know about ___?

5. What doesn't make sense to you?

To associate:

1. What are you thinking about right now? Why?

2. What does this story remind you of? Are there events that are similar to another story or to events in your life (compare-O-graph)?

3. Who does this character remind you of? Is this character similar to another character you know in another story or in real life (compare-O-graph)?

To notice:

1. What is an interesting description that you noticed?

2. What new or interesting words did you notice?

3. What important story clue did you notice?

To elaborate:

1. How might you make that sentence more interesting?

2. What kind of character would you add to the story?

To predict-verify-decide:

1. What's going to happen next?

2. What are some important clues (predict-O-graph)?

3. How do you think this story will end?

To infer:

1. What does this tell us about that character?

2. Based on story clues, what do you think happened before or what do you think will happen next?

3. How does ___ feel about ___?

To imagine or visualize:

1. What do you image this (person, place, or thing) looks like?

2. What does this scene look like to you? What are some things you would see if you were there? What picture is painted in your mind?

To summarize:

1. What are the important events that have happened so far?

2. What's happened so far? Who did what?

To decide:

1. What do you think ___ should do?

2. How might ___ solve this problem?

3. What would you do if you were ___?

Figure 5.6   Questions for Shared Reading: Expository Text

To preview:

1. What do you think this chapter or article is about? What clues do you see in the title or cover of the book?
2. What does the title tell us?
3. What are some interesting things you see on the cover of the book?

To check for understanding:

1. What is this chapter about?
2. What are 3 important ideas?
3. What do you want to know more about?
4. What do I know about ___?
5. Should we reread the paragraph?

To elaborate and connect:

1. How might you restate that sentence?
2. How could that be stated more clearly?
3. How might you make that sentence more interesting?

Questions for during reading:

1. What things are a little fuzzy?
2. How else do you think ___ could be applied?
3. How could ___ be changed, modified, or elaborated?
4. What are the main parts of ___?
5. How would you compare this to ___?
6. What's the main idea in this paragraph?

To summarize:

1. What are the important ideas so far?
2. What do you hope to learn more about?
3. How would you explain ___?
4. How would you define ___?

Figure 5.7   Bloom's Taxonomy and Related Action Words

Bloom's Taxonomy

1. **Knowledge Level Operations.** Define, describe, identify, list, match, name, tell, show, label, collect, examine, tabulate, quote, duplicate, memorize, recognize, relate, recall, repeat, reproduce, or state.

2. **Comprehension Level Operations.** Interpret, explain, summarize, convert, distinguish, estimate, generalize, rewrite, contrast, predict, associate, differentiate, discuss, extend, classify, express, indicate, locate, report, restate, review, select, or translate.

3. **Application Level Operations.** Apply, change, compute, demonstrate, operate, show, use, solve, calculate, complete, illustrate, examine, modify, relate, change, classify, experiment, dramatize, employ, interpret, operate, practice, schedule, sketch, or write.

4. **Analysis Level Operations.** Identify parts, distinguish, diagram, outline, relate or associate, break down, subdivide, analyze, separate, order, explain, classify, arrange, divide, select, explain, infer, analyze, calculate, categorize, compare, contrast, differentiate, discriminate, examine, question, or test.

5. **Synthesis Level Operations.** Combine, compose, create, design, rearrange, integrate, modify, substitute, plan, invent, formulate, prepare, generalize, or rewrite.

6. **Evaluation Level Operations.** Appraise, criticize, compare and contrast, support, conclude, discriminate, find important points, infer, deduce, assess, decide, rank, grade, test, measure, recommend, convince, select, explain, discriminate, support, argue, choose, compare, defend, estimate, judge, predict, rate, select, value, or evaluate.

Last Word

This chapter described three lesson formats. The SRE lesson is used to enable students to read text independently. The following pre-reading strategies are described for use with this format:

- Story preview
- Story map
- Relevant schemata
- Background information
- Character analysis
- Story grammar
- Important vocabulary words
- Advanced organizers
- Short related discussion

The guided reading lesson is used to teach specific skills within an authentic reading context. The specific steps for planning this type of lesson were described earlier in the chapter.

The shared reading lesson is designed to enable readers of varying levels to have a shared discussion around a common text. Specific discussion questions for use with both narrative and expository text are listed here. The following during-reading strategies were also described:

- ERT
- Every-other

Section III

10 Instructional Elements

6

10 Elements of Reading Instruction

> *Give a teacher a basal and that teacher will know what to do for a few students today. Give a teacher an understanding of the literacy learning process and that teacher will know what to do for all students for a long time.*

NO MAGICAL PROGRAMS

When I first started working with students with severe reading difficulties, I was a bit overwhelmed. Where do you start when you have an eighth- or ninth-grade student reading at the first-grade level? What exactly do you do with a second-grade student who is in a constant state of reading failure? I wanted the security of some sort of program that would tell me exactly what to do. However, such programs do not exist. There's not a singular approach or type of instruction that works best for all students who are struggling to learn to read (Allington, 2005). Yet time and money continue to be spent on commercial programs using a singular approach. These programs lack both supporting research and success for students with reading difficulties (Coles, 2003).

If indeed there were a single best method for teaching reading that worked best for all students all the time, I'd have titled this book *The Best Method for Teaching Reading.* But I didn't. Humans aren't standardized products. Our brains all function a little bit differently. We all learn a little bit differently. And since humans aren't standardized products, we cannot expect there to be a standardized process to effectively teach these very unstandardized humans to read.

COMPREHENSIVE READING INSTRUCTION

To be effective, any approach to reading instruction should enable teachers to make choices based on the needs, interests, and strengths of the students with whom they are working. As well, instruction should be multidimensional, it should recognize many different ways of thinking and types of intelligence, and it should be fairly simple and easy to use. Finally, it should be validated by a wide variety of research from different perspectives. These are all characteristics of what I call Comprehensive Reading Instruction (CRI) or when used as an intervention, Comprehensive Reading Intervention.

There is nothing new or overly complicated about CRI. Teachers don't need to pay hundreds of dollars to get special training by certified trainers in order to use it. School districts don't need to spend taxpayer money to have some big shot come in and explain the program (although my schedule is wide open). Note: If any educational method is so complicated that teachers need to get special training to use it, it most likely is a mirage. Sadly, there is a vast educational consulting market built on this mirage (Coles, 2003; Garan, 2005). All you need to do to effectively meet the needs of struggling readers (or any reader) is attend to the 10 essential instructional elements listed on the following page. No single element by itself is effective. Instead, the 10 elements work together holistically. Thus, they should all be included, to some degree, in any curriculum or instructional plan for students with reading difficulties.

The chapters that follow describe strategies for each of the 10 essential elements. Attend to all elements, not in one session but over time. Adopt and adapt strategies from each elemental area as you see fit. Use only the ones that seem to work for you and your students. Keep in mind that students will vary in how much they need from each element. Here's a good rule of the thumb: If it seems to work, keep doing it. If it doesn't seem to work, tweak it or try something else. Keep it simple. Learning to read is very much like learning to play the piano in that progress occurs with practice over time.

10 Essential Elements for Reading Instruction

Remember, reading is creating meaning with print. Effective reading teachers do not teach students how to read. Instead, effective reading teachers create the conditions whereby all students can develop their ability to create meaning with print. Below are the 10 elements that are essential for creating these conditions.

1. **Concepts of print** examples include what a book is, the meaning of words, the sounds of letters, combining letters to create words, and reading print from left to right. Instruction here usually occurs only at the emergent levels (in preschool and early kindergarten).

2. **Phonemic awareness** is the ability to hear and manipulate the sounds within words. Strategies here include breaking words into parts based on sounds, identifying specific sounds within words, and manipulating sounds to create words (see Chapter 7). In general, phonemic awareness activities should be discontinued once students are reading comfortably at the first- grade level.

3. **Emotion and motivation** is perhaps the most important element when working with students who are struggling readers (Johnson, 2012). This element is related to the desire to read and the affective or emotional element surrounding reading (see Chapter 8). Often students who are struggling readers have encountered a whole lot of failure, frustration, and humiliation in their school experience. Reading and reading instruction can easily become associated with these very negative experiences. Strategies here include proximal instruction, scaffolded activities, and creating a positive emotional climate.

4. **Literature** refers to providing books and other material that students want to read. It's very hard for students to feel motivated to read if they don't have quality books at the appropriate reading level. This element focuses on providing quality reading material, as well as creating the conditions necessary to make reading enjoyable (see Chapter 9).

5. **Phonics** is the ability to associate sounds with letters or letter patterns (see Chapter 10).

6. **Word identification strategies and skills** are the strategies and skills students' use to identify words as they are reading. There are six general types of word identification skills: (a) analogy (word families), (b) morphemic awareness (prefix, suffix, affix, root), (c) context clues—semantics, (d) sight words, (e) syntax, and (f) phonics (see Chapter 11).

Instruction related to phonics and word identification should be discontinued as word identification strategies when students are reading comfortably at the third-grade level; however, word identification strategies should be continued as part of vocabulary development.

7. **Fluency** is the ability to process text quickly and efficiently. Fluency is highly correlated with comprehension and reading volume. Strategies here are designed to strengthen neural pathways in order to enhance the processing of text (see Chapter 12).

8. **Comprehension** includes the specific comprehension skills students use to understand expository text. It also includes strategies to develop the cognitive processes used to comprehend narrative text (see Chapters 13 and 14).

9. **Vocabulary** in reading is the number of words students know. The focus here is on enhancing both receptive and productive vocabularies. Strategies are designed to add depth and dimension to students' knowledge of words (see Chapter 15).

10. **Writing** enhances students' ability to read. It helps develop phonetic awareness as well as syntactic and semantic cueing systems (all essential components in identifying words during reading). Instruction here should focus on the process of writing (prewriting, drafting, revising, and editing) as well as the product or mechanical elements (grammar, punctuation, and spelling) (see Chapter 16). However, in the context of reading instruction, writing activities are often simplified.

TEACHING READING WITH THE BRAIN IN MIND

The focus of this book is on brain-friendly approaches for helping students learn to read. According to Eric Jensen (2005), there are seven critical factors that should be addressed in brain-based approaches to teaching and learning: (1) engagement, (2) repetition, (3) input quantity, (4) coherence, (5) timing, (6) error corrections, and (7) emotional states. Each of these is described here along with its application to reading instruction.

1. Engagement

Learning of any kind is most efficient when relevant neural networks are engaged, resulting in focused attention. The following are tips for enhancing focused attention:

• **Reduce the length of time required for focused attention during instruction**. Figure 6.1 shows Jensen's recommendations for the duration of direct instruction (2005). Outside of this, learning is reduced significantly. Direct and explicit instruction is necessary for students who are struggling readers (Wharton-McDonald, 2011); however, this instruction should be brief and briskly paced, followed by strategies that get students actively involved. The strategy could be as simple as "turn to a neighbor and share an important idea." The point is, the brain learns best when instruction is provided in smaller bits instead of large blobs, followed by a chance to do something with the new instructional input. The essence of good teaching is this: say a little bit, do a little bit.

• **Include the least amount of instruction necessary**. Students do not learn to read by listening to you tell them things. Create the conditions for authentic reading and writing experiences, and then get out of the way.

• **Use relevant tasks and activities**. Design literacy experiences in which students are able to read, explore, and discuss issues of

Figure 6.1   Appropriate Amount of Direction Instruction

Grade Level	Duration
K–2	5–8 minutes
3–5	8–12 minutes
6–8	12–15 minutes
9–12	12–15 minutes
Adults	15–18 minutes

relevance to them. Also, use writing prompts and activities that enable students to describe their ideas and experiences.

• **Allow students to make choices about books to read or writing topics.**

• **Provide time and space for students to become engrossed in reading and writing**. Use block scheduling with older students. For younger students, once they have become engaged in the act of reading or writing, leave them alone. Resist the need to move on. Getting students fully engaged in authentic literacy tasks is the very apex of reading instruction.

2. Repetition

Human brains are not like computers where you input data once and it is stored and retrieved exactly as you input it. Human brains need to touch skills and concepts repeatedly in order to strengthen neural pathways and build neural networks. Here are two tips:

• **Use pre-reading activities that give students a sense of what they will read or learn.** Use post-reading activities in which students engage with the salient elements of the text or lesson. These are both forms of repetition.

• **Review, revisit, and reinforce often.** You cannot teach a literacy skill once and expect student mastery. You have to review and revisit skills many times, in different ways, and at successively higher levels over time for real learning to occur. This is especially true with struggling readers who often have difficulties with letter-sound patterns. For example, when teaching a phonogram or a particular letter-sound relationship, introduce it initially using direct instruction, but then review it in subsequent days using a variety of strategies including cloze, maze, fluency activities, riddles, writing, and other creative activities. Also, use posters, sponge activities, games, and quick 5- to 30-second minilessons throughout the year to review skills learned.

3. Input Quantity

The human brain can learn a lot over time but only a little at one time. In-depth learning requires time for organizing, integrating, and storing new information. It is much easier to process and encode new information when it is presented in small, meaningful chunks. Here are four tips:

• **Slow down your rate of instruction**. There is a tendency, when students seem not to be grasping a skill or concept, to want to give them more input at a faster rate. However, more learning usually occurs when fewer things are presented and practiced more in-depth.

• **Insert pause and process (P&P) time into instruction** (see Figure 6.2). Instead of constant exposure to a single instructional element, use brief bits of instruction or instructional activities with small bits of P&P time. Students need this to think about and fully process your instructional input. Inserting small breaks into your lesson will enable students to engage all parts of the brain and to integrate new information with knowledge already stored in long-term memory. Effective P&P is intentional and planned.

Figure 6.2   Typical Instructional Session With P&P

P&P time need not be complicated; just a small space where students do not have to hold full concentration. It allows time for them to process the input or activity without becoming totally disengaged. It could be as simple as a 5 to 10 second pause before saying, "Alright. That was our cloze activity. You did a pretty great job on that today. You were able to fill in the blanks." Pause for another 5 to 10 seconds, then say, "Let's move to our fluency work."

1. Language experience: 5–8 minutes, P&P

2. Scaffolded writing: 3–5 minutes, P&P

3. Word work: 3–5 minutes, P&P

4. Cloze: 2–3 minutes, P&P

5. Fluency work: 3–5 minutes, P&P

6. Scaffolded reading practice or guided reading: 5–8 minutes, P&P

7. Comprehension work: 2–4 minutes, P&P

8. Game: 3–5 minutes

P&P could also be a more formalized activity such as a game, discussion, journal writing, or small group activity.

• **Use distributed practice**. Students are more apt to stay fully engaged and will learn more if you distribute 15 minutes of instructional input into three 5-minute segments dispersed over 20 minutes instead of 15 minutes of massed instructional input followed by 5 minutes of downtime. In behavioral and cognitive psychology, this is known as distributed practice versus massed practice (Ormand, 2012). The same amount of instructional input time is used in both cases; however, it is much easier to process and encode small, meaningful chunks of information than a massive blob of input. Figure 6.2 provides a sense of content and pace that could be used in a 40- to 60-minute reading intervention session.

• **Slow down but move quickly from one thing to the next**. This is not as paradoxical as it sounds. Your actual instruction should be at a pace at which students can fully understand and process the content. This usually means including less content in each instructional session, but if you slow things down too much, students will become bored and disengage. You have to find that just-right, Goldilocks zone. This means you need to watch your students and move quickly from one thing to the next thing when you sense they are ready to move on.

4. Coherence

Our brains naturally try to see patterns and make sense out of the world we encounter. It is a meaning-making organ that strives to find the logical consistency in all the stimuli that bombards us at any given moment. In reading instruction you can enhance this natural inclination by tapping into prior knowledge and by identifying the structure of what is to be read or learned.

• **Activate relevant schemata.** Prior knowledge influences what we perceive and how we interpret new information. When reading informational text, find out what students know about the concepts to be read. Brainstorm and list these known things on the board as a pre-reading activity that will activate relevant schemata. You may also need to do some preteaching that links new concepts to known concepts.

• **Use advanced organizers.** These are pre-reading activities that show students the structure of what they will be reading. If reading informational text, show students the salient elements in outline form, as they will be encountered in the text. If reading narrative text, show some or all of the story grammar elements (characters, events, and settings).

5. Timing

Our brains do not operate at peak efficiency all the time. We have peaks and valleys throughout the day. Also, different students are best able to concentrate and learn at varying parts of the day. Finally, it is natural for individual students' performance to vary from day to day.

- **Vary the times of reading instruction**. You might teach reading at 9:00 one day, 10:30 the next day, and 2:00 the next. Such a schedule widens the possibilities of catching students operating at peak cognitive efficiency.

- **Remind parents and students that brains need sleep to operate efficiently**. Adolescents tend to be sleep deprived. This makes learning of any kind difficult.

- **Get physical.** Use activity shifts, movement, and stand and stretch breaks within the classroom and within the teaching or learning session to stimulate the brain.

6. Error Correction

Trial and error learning is how our brain learns best. For learning, we need to be able to mess around, get feedback, and make corrections.

- **Allow students time to make self-corrections during oral reading**. Do not immediately correct mistakes, or try to explain to students how to sound out words. Teach them to pause, and see if the sentence or paragraph makes sense.

- **Use cloze activities** (see Chapter 11). Here students see a sentence with a word missing. This is a type of problem solving that is used to develop students' ability to use context to identify words.

- **As a post-reading activity, create sentences related to the story in which one word does not belong or fit**. Students must read the sentence, find the word, and replace it with a word that fits. This activity works best in pairs or small groups because the conversation that takes place creates a deeper level of learning.

- **Use word sorts**. These activities require inductive analysis in which students look at a field and try to induce order on the field by putting things in groups. Here students are given 10 to 20 words.

They are asked to create groups according to letter patterns (phonetic cueing system) or meaning (vocabulary). Again, this works best if done in pairs or small groups.

• **Make predictions**. In making predictions, students identify clues to determine what might happen next in a story. Create activities where students are able make predictions both before and during the reading of narrative texts, then check their predictions (see Chapter 13).

• **Use a pre-post chart**. Pre-post is a variation on the traditional KWL and works best with expository text. Here students identify and list what they know about a topic before reading (see Figure 6.3). I usually ask for a specific number depending on the age of the students. Example: "Tell me three things you know about bumble bees." This can be done in a large group, small group, or individually. After reading, students identify things to add in the second column.

Figure 6.3   Pre-Post Chart

Pre: What do you know?	Post: What can you add?
1.	1.
2.	2.
3.	3.

7. Emotional States

Students' emotional states are a significant variable for learning (Hinton, Miyamota, & Dell-Chiese, 2008). In my work with students who are struggling readers, I have found this to be the most significant variable (see Chapter 8). Emotions influence how and what we perceive and how we reconstruct and remember things (Sousa, 2012). Positive emotional states enhance learning. Negative emotional states detract from learning. Much of brain-based teaching involves creating positive states in which students are motivated and want to learn. Here are four tips:

• **Reduce the threat of failure or embarrassment**.
• **Use scaffolding to enable students to experience success**.

- **Include games and other fun activities to create positive emotional states**. Games can reinforce learning and at the same time create positive emotional states. Conclude each teaching session with a game so that students have something to look forward to.
- **Include social interaction**. We are a social species. Our brains evolved to interact with other humans. Use this natural inclination by including activities in which students interact with other students.

Last Word

In this chapter, I provided a brief overview of the 10 essential elements for reading instruction. I also presented strategies and recommendations that addressed seven critical factors related to brain-based teaching and learning. The remainder of this book will be devoted to describing a variety of research-based strategies for helping students develop their abilities to create meaning with print.

7

Emergent Literacy

Concepts of Print
and Phonemic Awareness

*It's not the "what" of phonics that's in question;
it's the "how" and the "how much" where people
have differing views.*

The first part of this chapter provides a sense of what effective literacy instruction might look like at the preschool and kindergarten (emergent) levels. At the end of this chapter, I describe seven phonemic-phonics hybrid activities that would be appropriate for some older students.

APPROACHES TO
EARLY LITERACY INSTRUCTION

In the Introduction, I described two general approaches to reading instruction: the code-first and meaning-first approaches. In this chapter, these two approaches will be shown in the context of early literacy instruction (students ages three, four, and five).

Code First

The code-first approach, sometimes called the *reading readiness approach,* assumes that children require a great deal of explicit instruction in order to be made ready to read. Direct instruction is used to teach a prescribed set of reading subskills (such as alphabetics, phonics, and phonemic awareness), in a predetermined order (scope and sequence), using predominately drill and practice.

There are some effective elements to take from this approach; however, research to support the efficacy of skills-only, phonics-first programs at the emergent level is inconclusive (Cole, 2003; Pearson & Hiebert, 2013; Smith, 2003). While instruction that focuses solely on reading subskills may result in increases in measures of these same reading subskills initially (as we would expect), it has not been shown to demonstrate positive effects on oral reading, comprehension, word recognition, or spelling at the emergent level (Casbergue & McGee, 2011; Cain, 2009; Paciga, Hoffman, & Teale, 2011; Taylor, Anderson, Au, & Raphael, 2000) or on higher-level literacy skills and later literacy achievement (Teale, Hoffman, & Paciga, 2010). As well, these types of interventions do not reflect what we know about human learning and how the brain creates meaning. Finally, this approach does not give any attention to young children's social, emotional, cognitive, or physical development.

Meaning First

The meaning-first approach, sometimes called an *emergent literacy approach,* assumes that literacy emerges as a series of skills and behaviors that develop naturally as children are developmentally ready and as they are exposed to certain conditions. This emergence occurs in much the same way that oral language emerges. This approach is based in large part on observations of real children actually learning within natural settings (Cambourne, 1993; Clay, 1982; Piaget & Inhelder, 1969; Vygotsky, 1978). Meaning-first approaches have been shown to outperform code-first approaches in measures of reading comprehension, writing, and metacognitive knowledge (Yaden, Rowe, & MacGillivray, 2000).

Meaning-first approaches tend to align with our natural human tendencies for language learning. In this sense, humans are naturally hardwired to learn language (Chomsky, 1968). The same language acquisition device the brain uses to learn to speak is involved in learning to read and write. Young children learn to speak because

- they're immersed in actual, real-life speaking experiences,
- they're provided small bits of instruction in authentic contexts,
- they're encouraged to talk about things that make sense and are of interest to them,
- they use language for real-life purposes.
- we respond to them instead of correcting them,
- we encourage their early attempts and successful approximations, and
- language is used in play and social interactions.

In effective meaning-first classrooms, these same conditions are applied to learning to read and write. Thus, we don't teach children to read and write as much as we create the conditions whereby all students can develop their full-literacy capacities. This occurs when children are engaged in authentic literacy experiences with explicit instruction, modeling, and scaffolding and with lots of time to practice reading and writing. (These same conditions should be applied to literacy learning at all levels.) Figure 7.1 contains elements that Morrow and Dougherty (2011) have identified as being essential for effective literacy instruction in preschool and kindergarten classrooms.

Figure 7.1   Elements Necessary for Effective
              Emergent Literacy Instruction

- explicit modeling and scaffolding of lesson to be learned
- guided practice
- independent practice
- time on task
- structure and routines
- differentiation of instruction to meet individual needs
- feedback for children
- time to explore
- time to experiment
- time to collaborate in social settings
- time for problem solving

Skills Instruction in a Meaning-First Approach

Meaning-first approaches to early literacy instruction use direct and explicit instruction to teach reading subskills such as alphabetics, phonics, and phonemic awareness. However, these subskills are taught in ways that are developmentally appropriate and in the context of authentic reading and writing. Whereas a skills-based approach starts with explicit instruction of reading subskills and moves to real reading and writing later on, a meaning-first approach immerses students in authentic reading and writing experiences first, then teaches essential skills within that context. This actually results in more direct instruction than a skills-based approach. Here the necessary skills are taught directly in the context in which they are used. Also, students are not asked to make a link between abstract skills taught in one context and real-life literacy in another context. Figure 7.2 contains an example of the types of instruction and activities that might be used with a meaning-first approach in a kindergarten classroom.

Figure 7.2   An Example of the Types of Activities
Used in a Meaning-First Approach

Mr. Jay is a kindergarten teacher. He introduces the letter /b/ within the context of a big book about bees. Children are asked to draw the letter /b/ in the air. As the class reads the book together, Mr. Jay points to each word with a pointer as it is read. He asks children to keep an eye out for words that begin with the /b/ sound. After each page he asks the children if they heard any /b/ words.

After reading the book about bees, Mr. Jay and the children write a list with three things to remember about bees. He asks the children for their ideas and writes sentences in large letters on a poster so that the children can hear and see him write. After each sentence, the children use choral reading to read each sentence two or three times. Volunteers are asked to come up and point to the /b/ words. They save their bee word list to practice reading the next day. Throughout the day or week, he might do any of the following types of activities:

- After a short minilesson showing pictures with words written underneath that begin with the /b/ sound, children are given a picture-word, many of which begin with the /b/ sound. Mr. Jay has a /b/ house on a bulletin board. Children are asked to come up front and show their picture-word to the class and decide if it goes into the /b/ house. He pins the /b/ picture-word in that house.

(Continued)

(Continued)

- Children do predictable writing about things that are big. On the poster, there are sentences for each child with that child's name behind it. Each child is asked to name something that's big. The teacher writes it in the blank. Children then reread the poster in order to practice reading about things that are big.

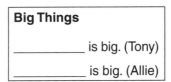

- After a short lesson on the front carpet about bees, children write their own bee stories. The class generates three to five words that would complete the sentence: Bees are ____. Mr. Jay writes these on the board. Children finish the sentence for their bee story using one of the words on the board (or their own), then draw a picture above it.

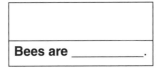

- For playtime, there are many objects and games that begin with the letter /b/. Mr. Jay introduces these before play time and writes the word on a board or poster.
- Mr. Jay uses games, songs, riddles, art projects, and even dances that incorporate words with the letter /b/. With each, he uses short one or two minute minilessons to reteach and reinforce the letter-sound relationship.

Mr. Jay is taking a systematic approach to letter sounds in that he starts with consonants and then moves to vowels. He checks off on his phonics checklist (see Chapter 10 Appendix, page 134) each time he teaches a particular letter sound. He also keeps a portfolio for each child and checks and writes the date when the child has mastered each skill.

Learning letter-sound relationships is necessary for learning to read but far from sufficient. Learning to read and write cannot be reduced to simply mastering a predefined set of subskills. Instead, early literacy learning is more like systems theory in that there is an interrelationship among multiple elements: linguistic, cognitive, emotional, and social systems (Dickinson, McCabe, & Essex, 2006), as well as knowledge and experience (Neuman, 2006). Each element reinforces as well as draws upon the other. Thus, an effective meaning-first approach focuses on nurturing and developing each of these elements in developmentally appropriate ways.

Developmentally Appropriate Instruction

There is a reason why effective kindergarten instruction does not look like instruction in a first-grade classroom: kindergarten is not first grade. There are certain types of instruction and experiences that are very effective for older students but that are simply not developmentally appropriate for young children (International Reading Association and the National Association for the Education of Young Children, 1998). Thus, with young children you want to avoid what is called the *push-down curriculum.* This is where a first-grade curriculum gets pushed down into kindergarten or preschool.

Children think in qualitatively different ways at different stages of development. Thus, instruction for young children must be developmentally appropriate. Starting reading instruction sooner doesn't mean students will be further ahead at a later point. From a developmental standpoint, educational experiences must fit students' social, emotional, cognitive, and physical developmental levels. This doesn't mean that you shouldn't address phonics and other reading subskills in preschool and kindergarten classrooms. It means that the form that this instruction takes should be developmentally appropriate. It's not the "what" of phonics as much as the "how" or the "how much" that is in question. Worksheets and a lot of time spent drilling and practicing are not developmentally appropriate practices at the emergent levels. Most instruction at these levels should be incidental or involve play. This is how young children learn.

Whole-to-Part-to-Whole Instruction

Learning complex skills (such as reading and writing) is most efficient when addressed whole-to-part-to-whole (Donnelly & Davidoff, 1999; Helmut, 2005; Julia, 2006; Lim, Reiser, & Olina, 2009; Tanaka & Gauthier 1997). When learners can get a sense of the whole, they're better able to see where the smaller parts fit within this context. The description of Mr. Jay in Figure 7.2 is an example of whole-to-part-to-whole instruction. Children here were immersed in authentic reading and writing experiences (whole). They were given small bits of letter-sound instruction (part) within this meaningful context. They were then invited to engage in other authentic literacy experiences (whole). For example, they would spend time each day reading real books. Their reading at this level may rely more on picture cues than letter cues, but they were creating meaning with print. Activities here would include picture reading, pretend reading, echo reading, and choral reading. Mr. Jay also tried to get children to write real things. Again, their writing may rely more on pictures than letters, but they were using pictures and letter symbols to communicate in developmentally appropriate ways.

CREATING THE CONDITIONS FOR EARLY LITERACY LEARNING

So what does effective literacy instruction look like in a preschool or kindergarten setting? Described below are some of the developmentally appropriate practices you might see. This is by no means an exhaustive or complete list, but it should provide you with a sense of the types of activities that are appropriate for literacy learners at this level.

1. **Lots of Talk**. Teachers should be having conversations with children and directing their conceptual learning, as well as introducing new words into their vocabulary. Oral-language ability, vocabulary, and general knowledge are strong predictors of reading achievement and comprehension in the later grades (Biemiller, 2006; Neuman, 2006). Thus, there should be individual and large group teacher-directed conversations as well as structured and unstructured opportunities for children to interact with other children. Also, small bits of teaching, both planned and incidental, provide rich opportunities to build students' knowledge base and vocabulary.

2. **Lots of Reading.** This reading should take a variety of forms. Foremost are teachers reading books with children. These provide opportunities for incidental learning about words and concepts found in the book. This is also the place for the incidental teaching of phonemic awareness and phonics skills. Example: "Boys and girls, this story is called, 'Big Bunny.' See the 'B'? It makes the 'buh' sound like ball and boy."

There should be narrative texts (stories) as well as expository text (informational books). The classroom should be filled with lots of good books on a variety of subjects. Big books are used as well, with the teacher pointing to individual words as they are read. Sometimes children read along with the teacher (choral reading), other times the teacher reads a line of text and then the children read it back (echo reading). The teacher should also model the reading of lists, signs, and environmental print. There is picture reading where children read or retell a story using the pictures in the book. Children are provided lots of opportunities to talk about and explore books. Finally, there should be recorded books on CD or on the Internet that students can listen to. There should be headphones available. With Internet texts, look for books that highlight the words as they are read to the student.

3. **Lots of Writing.** Large group writing should involve language experience activities where students are asked for ideas and the teacher records their ideas on a poster or board (see Chapter 9). Example: "Boys and girls, yesterday we went to the zoo. What should we say about that in our morning letter? Who has an idea?" The teacher then writes down what the student says, saying each word as she or he writes so students can see the letter-sound connection. You want students to read short, grammatically correct sentences. Thus, it is acceptable to paraphrase and edit. Choral reading or echo reading is then used to practice fluency and word identification skills. As will be shown in other places in the book, language experience activities are an excellent place for short, phonics minilessons.

Knowing that writing develops in stages, there should be lots of paper, pencils, white boards, and or other writing utensils lying around for children to mess around with and explore. Allowing time and opportunity for children to explore enhances the development of their literacy skills.

Figure 7.3   Examples of Driting

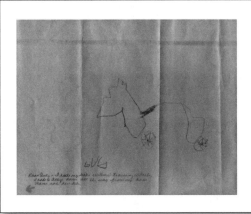

Early writing takes the form of "driting". This is a combination of drawing and writing. In writing a letter or story, the child starts with a drawing. The teacher asks the child, "Tell me about your story." The teacher writes what the child says on the picture. When the child proudly takes the letter or story home, it is used to practice reading. On the previous page, in Figure 7.3, are some early examples of driting letters sent to me by my nephews.

Writing can also take the form of predictable writing or stories (see Chapter 16). Here an open-ended sentence is written or printed with a space for students' individual responses (see Figure 7.4). Student responses can be dictated or you can encourage them to write. These words are printed on top of the chart enabling all students to be successful. At the same time, you are reinforcing letter sounds. This is a form of scaffolding. It provides students the structure necessary to be successful when they read it back.

Figure 7.4   Examples of Predictable Writing

I like to eat _____	My name is _____
I like to eat _____	My name is _____
I like to eat _____	My name is _____

The teacher should model writing whenever possible to students. Lists or reminders work well here. Example: "Boys and girls, I need to remind myself to take my apple to lunch. What should I write?" As students provide an idea, the teacher writes it on the board, sounding out each word as it is written. You can also model writing posters and signs. The point is, students see you using writing for real purposes. You are able to teach and reinforce words and letter sounds in authentic, meaningful writing contexts.

4. **Play.** Play is how children come to know the world. It is the best modality for learning at the emergent level. Play should be used to both introduce and reinforce skills and concepts. For example, when teaching the /b/ sound, toys or objects that start with the letter /b/ would be labeled and featured. When teaching a unit on birds, a teacher might have toys or figures related to birds that children can play with. Games in which children have to match an object and pictures with letter sounds are effective. Play could also involve flashcards and simple Ipad and computer games.

5. **Planned, systematic, direct, and explicit phonics instruction.**
This may seem contradictory to the meaning-first approach described
above, but remember, it's not the "what" of phonics; it's the "how"
and the "how much" of phonics that is important. It is effective to
systematically work your way through all the letter sounds using
short bits of explicit instruction (30 seconds to no more than four or
five minutes), followed by play or other creative and developmentally appropriate activities to reinforce the letter sound. It's systematic
because you keep a chart, making note of the skills taught and the
date (see Chapter 10 Appendix, page 134). You also keep a chart or
checklist to record when you notice students' mastering each subskill.
Not only are you using direct instruction here, but you are using a
very direct form of assessment. This same approach can be taken with
sight words, phonograms, and phonemic awareness skills.

CONCEPTS OF PRINT

As described in the last chapter, concepts of print include examples
such as what a book is, words have meaning, letters stand for sounds,
letters are put together to create words, and print is read from left to
right. These concepts are learned in the early years (birth through age
three) as children interact naturally with an adult around books and
other forms of print in literate environments. Very little, if any, direct
instruction should be used here. However, we must make sure parents understand the importance of talking with and reading to their
young children because these early literacy experiences have a positive impact on children's cognitive and language development, reading skills, and school achievement (Britto, Fuligni, & Brooks-Gunn,
2006). This also points to the importance of programs such as Early
Head Start in helping to insure that all children come to school reading and able to learn.

PHONEMIC-PHONICS HYBRID ACTIVITIES

The terms *phonological awareness*, *phonemic awareness*, and *phonics* are
often confused.

Phonological awareness refers to the ability to focus on the
sound of speech, as well as intonation, rhythm, syllables, and
rhyme. Phonemic awareness is the ability to hear and manipulate
individual phonemes within words. *Phonemes* are the smallest units
of sound within spoken words. English has 41 to 44 phonemes.

Phonemic awareness is purely auditory. *Phonics* refers to making letter-sound associations and using that knowledge to decode individual words.

Phonemic-Phonics Hybrids for Older Students

A rule of thumb is that phonemic awareness activities should generally be discontinued once children are reading comfortably at the first-grade level. However, some students with severe reading difficulties in later grades benefit from having phonemic awareness activities as part of their total reading program (as well as students whose first language may not be English). With these students, I have found that phonemic-phonics hybrid activities, such as those described below, tend to be more effective than just phonemic awareness activities.

1. **Phonemic Segmentation.** Here students break words into parts based on phonemes. First, the student hears the word and identifies each phonemic segment. For example, with the word pig the phonemic segments are the following: /p/, /i/, and /g/. Then, show students the complete word as well as the word broken into phonemic parts (see Figure 7.5). Next, the student reads the word and points to and identifies each phoneme: /p/, /i/, and /g/. Finally, the student rereads the complete word.

Figure 7.5 Phonemic Segmentation Based on the /ig/ Phonogram

| pig |
| p - i - g |
| pig |

This type of activity works well when presented on a screen or slide presentation. You can also create a paper version of this activity. Here students read across the page (see Figure 7.6).

Figure 7.6 Fast Phonemic Segmentation

may	m - ay	may
fill	f - i - ll	fill
fray	fr - ay	fray
mill	m - i - ll	mill
hay	h - a - y	hay
pill	p - i - ll	pill
play	pl - ay	play
still	st - i - ll	still

2. **Phoneme Categorization Activity.** Here students hear three words, two of which have similar sounds (see Figure 7.7). They are asked to identify the word in each set

Figure 7.7   Examples of Phoneme Categorization

Beginning Sounds	Middle Sounds	Ending Sounds
1. pay, pill, cram	1. cat, ham, hill	1. drip, mop, mat
2. cat, clam, hill	2. pay, pail, mat	2. cat, nut, bag
3. day, dill, rip	3. bill, tip, jet	3. grip, rap, set
4. sat, say, rip	4. snip, rip, cut	4. tug, big, sat
5. ray, ram, mat	5. day, sat, men	5. fill, pull, sat
6. play, pill, spat	6. lip, fill, light	6. tin, ran, sat
7. whip, will, hat	7. fray, mail, cub	7. hop, drip, mat
8. fill, fat, sip	8. cram, man, rate	8. sad, bed, rip
9. may, mat, bam	9. cat, jam, fill	9. lap, rip, exam
10. drill, drip, drop	10. dip, grill, dine	10. bunk, rink, cram

that has the "odd" sound. For example: "bun – bat – red. Which word does not belong with the other two?" Once students have identified the odd word, show them the three words and ask them to read the three words. Vary lessons using beginning, middle, and ending sounds.

3. **Phoneme Blending Activity.** Here students listen to a sequence of separately spoken phonemes and then combine them to form a word. Example: "What would you get if you put these sounds together /b/ - /i/ - /g/?" When students identify the word, show them the actual word.

4. **Phoneme Identification Activity.** Here students learn to recognize the same sounds in different words. Say three words with similar beginning, middle, or ending sounds (see Figure 7.8). Once students have identified the similar sound, show the three words. Then ask the students to point to the similar letter or cluster and read each word.

5. **Phoneme Addition Activity.** Here students make a new word by adding a phoneme to a phonogram. Example: "What word do you have if you add /s/ to the beginning of /ip/?" This is similar to the onset-rime or word building activities described in Chapter 10. The difference here is that you want to focus on sound or phonemes first, then show the letter patterns.

Figure 7.8 Phoneme Identification

Beginning Sounds	Middle Sounds	Ending Sounds
1. drill, drip, drop	1. hot, crop, sob	1. tank, bunk, rink
2. bay, bill, bat	2. sock, top, rob	2. bead, bed, had
3. day, dip, dam	3. hat, man, track	3. hip, mop, rap
4. tray, trip, trail	4. sip, hill, him	4. rain, man, pen
5. hay, hill, hip	5. stay, mail, pain	5. sob, blab, stub
6. Jill, jay, jam	6. bay, tail, stain	6. fill, hall, tell
7. tip, tag, tank	7. bill, stick, tin	7. mat, jet, hot
8. way, will, wag	8. bat, cram, tag	8. ram, dim, hum
9. fill, fat, fell	9. bell, head, nest	9. stag, rug, beg
10. spill, spat, spam	10. duck, cut, hum	10. track, stick, tuck

6. **Phoneme Isolation Activity.** Here students learn to recognize and identify individual sounds in a word. Example: "What is the first sound you hear in the work /sip/?" Here the student is not identifying a letter, rather a sound. "That's correct, the /s/ sound. The letter /s/ makes this sound." Do this for beginning, middle, and end sounds. Show the complete word only after students have identified the sound.

7. **Phoneme Substitution Activity.** Here students substitute one phoneme for another to make a new word. Example: Show and say the word /tip/. "What word would we get if we changed the /t/ sound in tip to a /r/ sound?" Make the /t/ and /r/ sounds for the student here. Show the new word after students have identified the word. Do this for the beginning, middle, and end sounds.

Last Word

This chapter examined two approaches to early literacy instruction. Most would agree that learning the subskills involved with reading is important. Where I differ from those who advocate a skills-based approach is that I believe that these subskills are necessary but far from sufficient. Learning to read and write cannot be reduced to simply mastering a predefined set of subskills. Instead, early literacy learning is more like systems theory in that there is an interrelationship among multiple elements: linguistic, cognitive, emotional, and social systems (Dickinson, McCabe, & Essex, 2006), as well as knowledge and experience (Neuman, 2006). Each element reinforces as well as draws upon the other. A meaning-first approach focuses on nurturing and developing each of these elements in developmentally appropriately ways.

This chapter ended by describing seven phonemic-phonics hybrid activities for older students that can be used to develop phonemic awareness and at the same time, reinforce letter-sound relationships:

- Phonemic segmentation
- Phoneme categorization activity
- Phoneme blending activity
- Phoneme identification activity
- Phoneme addition activity
- Phoneme isolation activity
- Phoneme substitution activity

8

Emotions and Motivation

> *"Welcome to school, Billy! Are you ready for another day of failing? Excellent!! At 9:00 you'll fail at reading. At 10:30 you'll fail at language arts. At 11:00 you'll fail at social studies, and at noon you'll hit a kid on the playground who teases you about failing and then spend the afternoon in the principal's office."*

Emotions and their derivative—motivation—are perhaps the most significant variables when working with any student, but especially students with reading difficulties, yet they seem to be given the least amount of attention.

EMOTIONS

We think, learn, and emote with the same brain. Thus, it would be silly to think that emotions would not be a factor in students' ability to learn. In fact, there's plenty of research to support the notion that positive emotional experiences can enhance learning and negative emotions can disrupt learning (Hinton, Miyamota, & Dell-Chiese,

2008; Johannessen & McCann, 2009; Machazo & Motz, 2005; Sousa, 2011). Attending to the emotional element is important in working with all students, but it is especially important when working with struggling readers (Hamre & Pianta, 2005; Van Ryzin, 2011).

Understanding

Try to understand what it must feel like to be a student who struggles with reading. First, think about how you react to failure and frustration. Then, try to imagine students in school settings where they encounter failure and frustration on a daily basis. They fail in a very public way. Every reading assignment is a reminder of what they're not able to do. They're given the not-too-subtle message that they are not very smart or that they can't learn. And sadly, after a while, many start to believe it.

Try to imagine what it must feel like. Think of a time in your life when you were a less-able learner, where you just could not learn the thing you were trying to learn. It may have been a sport, music or a musical instrument, tap dancing, algebra, statistics, physics, a foreign language, philosophy, or art. What did it feel like when everybody else seemed to learn easily while you did not? Were you motivated to come to class? Did you want to continue? Were you inspired to practice outside the teaching session? Did you enjoy doing what you could not do? Did you want to be "challenged"? Did you want somebody to quantify your performance and compare you to others?

Now try to imagine that you're an elementary student without the ability to sort through and analyze these feelings. Imagine you're a middle school student with very few experiences of success in academic settings. Imagine that you're a high school student who is hyperaware of what your peers think, say, and do. You're given the constant message that you don't measure up. Teachers assign daily reading and writing homework that overwhelms you and takes you three to four hours to complete each night. Then they infer that you're lazy or are not putting forth enough effort if you don't complete it. Imagine this.

Only by putting yourself in these situations can you begin to understand what students with reading difficulties feel like. Now you see why they might act out in class or have "behavior" problems (which are really feelings problems). You can begin to understand why it is that struggling readers sometimes shut down and put forth minimal effort and why they often hate school. Who wouldn't? It is a mistake to think these students don't want to learn. Instead, they don't want to fail, and their desire to not fail is much stronger than their desire to learn. However, if failure is the only option given to them, they will do everything possible to avoid the activity or show you how stupid the activity is in the first place.

> **Aside: Dealing With "Behavior" Problems.** Most behavior problems are really feelings problems. When schools focus only on behaviors, they're dealing with the effect but not the cause of the problem. Whether or not one is conscious of it, all actions arise from thoughts. Our thoughts are intricately linked with and directed by our emotions. You cannot effectively deal with negative behaviors without first dealing with the source of those negative behaviors. You cannot reward or punish your way into good behavior, only temporary compliance.

Honesty, Trust, and Relationship

In my work with struggling readers, I've found that the emotional component of reading and failing must be addressed first if you're going to make any progress. This component needs to be reinforced often to begin to counteract all the other negative and debilitating messages students receive during the day. You need to say very directly to the student, "You have trouble reading. It's not a big deal. It doesn't mean that you are dumb or can't learn. It just means that you have trouble reading. A lot of people have trouble reading. We're going to see what we can do to make it better." That's it: straight up, simple truth. This takes some of the pressure off the student.

Students also need to trust you. This means you have to establish some sort of trusting relationship. Establishing supportive, trusting relationships between teachers and learners has been shown to enhance all learning, including learning to read (Johannessen & McCann, 2009; Roger, Peck & Nasir, 2006; Van Ryzin, 2011). However, trust is earned, not given. Here are four basic tips:

1. **Don't frustrate students.** Don't put them in positions where they'll fail. Create activities and assignments that they can accomplish with teacher assistance (scaffolding).

2. **Use age appropriate instruction and reading materials.** Do not teach down to them. For older students, don't make them

read "ducky books." This is the term that I use for low-level books written for younger children.

3. **Listen**. Take an interest in their interests so that you can create literacy activities around their interests.

4. **Share yourself**. Real teaching starts with a relationship. Write and share some of your own stories with your students in order to establish a relationship.

THE VALUE-EXPECTANCY THEORY OF MOTIVATION

Source: Thinkstock/Jupiterimages.

Theories do not predict behavior; rather, they help us understand behavior. The value-expectancy theory of motivation is one such theory that can help us understand the behavior of struggling readers. This theory posits that students' motivation to engage in any behavior or activity is a result of how much they value the activity and their expectancy of success. Put this theory in a mathematical equation, and it looks like this: *value* x *expectancy* = *motivation*. Just like any multiplication equation, if one of the factors is zero, the product will be zero. Below, this theory is used to understand struggling readers' motivation to read and to engage in instructional activities related to reading.

Value

Is the activity or skill of any value to students? Do they find it of worth? Do they see themselves as using the skill in their everyday life? Is it enjoyable? Is it meaningful? There are three dimensions to value: (a) attainment value, (b) intrinsic value, and (c) utility value (Schunk & Zimmerman, 2006).

Attainment Value

Attainment value is the importance of having the skill or engaging in the activity. In reading, students most likely understand the utilitarian value of reading. They'd all like to be able to read and understand things. For older students, there's a strong desire to use email, texting, and other forms of social media to interact and socialize using the printed word. Since communicating with peers is very important, it would make sense to use this as the basis for literacy instruction with older students. This would help to enhance the attainment value of literacy.

Intrinsic Value

Intrinsic value is the amount of enjoyment derived from the task or skill. Do students find reading to be of interest? Is it enjoyable? It is very hard to value something that is meaningless, boring, and repetitive. Often reading instruction for students with reading disabilities is composed mostly of meaningless drill and practice on reading subskills. This makes reading abstract and disconnected from their human experience, as well as incredibly boring.

Also, it's hard to expect students to enjoy reading if they don't have something enjoyable to read. Students need lots of interesting things to read that are at their independent level or below. With adolescents, comic books and graphic novels are a very good source. The pictures make it interesting and help to carry the story. There is a lot of action, and there is minimal text to read on each page. These can be downloaded on a computer, Kindle, Ipad, or other devices.

Utility Value

Utility value is the perceived usefulness of the skill toward other goals. Do students need to use the skill? Is it useful in any way? This is why in literacy classes students should be engaged in authentic literacy experiences to the greatest degree possible. Authentic literacy experiences are where students read and write for real purposes—just like we do in the real world. Authentic literacy experiences include the following: reading for enjoyment or to get specific information; writing to record, organize, or convey their thoughts; and having real conversations about the books they've read and stories they've written. This is what we do as adults.

Expectancy

Too often the only thing struggling readers learn in reading class is how to fail. They've learned this lesson so well that they fail in most things related to literacy. Failure is not a great motivator. Nobody wants to do what he or she cannot do. Very few people want to be frustrated or embarrassed. Can you imagine a coach telling his or her team before a big game, "Okay team, let's go out there and fail miserably! Let's really embarrass ourselves in front of everybody this time! We can do it!"

Do struggling readers expect to succeed in the literacy learning tasks? *Self-efficacy* is the belief that you can accomplish what you set out to do. Research supports the notion that self-efficacy is strongly related to achievement (Schunk & Zimmeran, 2006; Sternberg & Williams, 2009; Wigfield, Byrnes, & Eccles, 2006). Things done to help develop self-efficacy are an important aspect of helping struggling readers learn to read. Frustrating students is a sure way to extinguish any remaining motivation there may have once been to read or learn to read.

SOME BASIC STRATEGIES

This section describes some basic strategies to use with struggling readers to enhance their motivation to read.

• **Engage in proximal instruction.** Struggling readers get frustrated by instruction that is too difficult for them. The result is learned helplessness. Instruction should be *proximal*. This means instruction should be in close proximity to students' ability to do the task independently. This instructional area, called the *zone of proximal development*, is just ahead of students' independent level, where they can accomplish a task with scaffolding or with teacher help (see Figure 8.1 on the next page). This is the Goldilocks zone: not too easy, not too hard, but just right.

Now I know you are saying to yourself, "Wait a minute, Dr. Johnson. I have 25 students in my class, all reading at different levels. How am I supposed to instruct in the Goldilocks zone?" Good question. You can't. Not with 25 students all at the same time. The one-size-fits all mode of instruction has never worked for teaching students to read (Allington, 2012). However, there are approaches to reading instruction like readers' workshop or Four Blocks™ (described in Chapter 9) that use flexible grouping to teach minilessons based on students' specific needs. These approaches also enable students to select books for reading practice that are of interest to them and are at the appropriate level.

• **Have easy and enjoyable books for students to read.** When you and I go to the library or bookstore, we don't look for books that challenge us. Instead, we look for books that we'll enjoy reading. Students should have the same option. Reading practice should be at students' independent level or below. There is no such thing as a book that is too easy when students are reading for enjoyment.

• **Provide choice.** When you and I go to a library or a bookstore nobody tells us what book we have to read. We get to choose.

Figure 8.1   Zone of Proximal Development

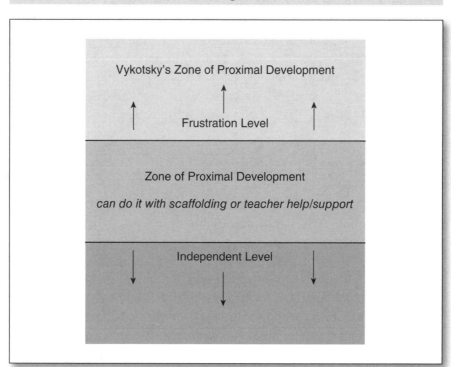

Why would we not want to offer students this same opportunity? Students should be able to make choices about the books they want to read. In the classroom, this does not mean total choice all the time. But neither does it mean no choice any of the time. The ideal is to provide the maximum choice possible while still maintaining academic and curricular goals. In the same way, students should be able to choose to stop reading a book that does not hold their interest when reading for enjoyment. Again, just like you and me, we do not force ourselves to read a book for enjoyment that we do not find enjoyable.

• **Make sure students experience success.** Every student needs to experience success. Experiencing success promotes self-efficacy, which is linked with student achievement. One way to do this is through various repeated reading activities where students are able to see their times improve after each attempt (see Chapter 12). Other ways are through scaffolded reading and writing activities, facilitated writing activities, shared reading, and class discussions. These are all ways to engage students in authentic literacy experiences while providing the structure necessary for them to succeed. Each of these strategies is described in this book.

- **Use scaffolded oral reading (ScORe).** Students with reading difficulties often need some sort of scaffolding to enable them to successfully engage in literacy experiences. ScORe is one such scaffold that can be used in large groups, small groups, or individually; however, it's most effectively used when working with individual students. ScORe is similar to the neurological impress method (Flood, Lapp, & Fisher, 2005). Here you and the student read the text together out loud. You act as a scaffold by reading a millisecond ahead of the student in order to maintain a steady, comfortable pace. If a student pauses or stumbles, you keep reading. The student will rely on your voice to act as a scaffold in identifying words during the process of reading. You should read using a quiet voice, providing just enough structure to keep the pace moving. If the student seems to be reading fluently, provide less scaffolding by sounding out just the beginning sounds of some words or by dropping out completely of others. Also, ScORe works best if you point to the words as you are reading them.

The goal again is to act as a scaffold to enable the student to read a book at a reasonable pace without having to stop to figure out words. This also allows the reader to enjoy reading without the cognitive demands that identifying words places on working memory.

- **Set small, attainable goals.** Make sure the initial goals you set with students are attainable. You can extend these later, but students need to experience success. They need to see that their effort has some sort of results. Figure 8.2 has examples of some of the types of initial goals you might use for students with severe reading difficulties.

- **Enable students to practice reading.** You learn to play the piano by daily practice. This is the way you develop those neural pathways

Figure 8.2 Examples of Initial Goals for Struggling Readers

1. Send two weekly emails or text messages.

2. Do four timed-reading activities during the week with a parent or friend (see Chapter 12).

3. Practice sight words with a parent or friend five times during the week.

4. Do a 10-minute listen and follow along with a recorded version of a book four times during the week.

5. Find one interesting comic strip to share.

and create new neural networks. You get better at playing tennis, baseball, dance, or whatever by daily practice. Let students know that it is the same way with reading. Keep reading practice short and focused initially. It is much better to have a 10-minute practice five times a week than a 30-minute practice twice a week.

• **Use scaffolded writing.** Writing is one of the best ways to enhance reading, as it strengthens syntactic and phonology cueing systems. To the greatest extent possible, allow students to choose their own writing topics. Students will be more motivated to write if they can select writing topics and express their ideas. Scaffolded writing activities are short, easy ways for students to express their ideas with structure or scaffolding provided by the teacher. These strategies are described in Chapter 16.

• **Include social interaction as part of instruction.** Students, especially adolescent students, are motivated when they can work in groups, communicate with each other, or have some sort of social interaction as part of instruction. Teaching is much easier and learning is greatly enhanced when we plan learning experiences that are aligned with students' natural tendencies and interests. As mentioned before, use all social media to teach and reinforce reading and writing. Design cooperative learning activities in which students who are struggling readers can still be successful. Create structured conversations around books and writing.

Last Word

This chapter looked at the effect of students' emotions on their learning. The value-expectancy theory was used to understand students' motivation. The following strategies were recommended:

- Engage in proximal instruction
- Have easy and enjoyable books for students to read
- Provide choice
- Make sure students experience success
- Use scaffolded oral reading (ScORe)
- Set small, attainable goals
- Enable students to practice reading
- Use scaffolded writing
- Include social interaction as part of instruction

9

Literature and Instructional Approaches

A reading teacher's number one job is to help students fall in love with books.

Of all the research-based strategies described in this book, wide reading is perhaps the most effective and the easiest to implement. Extensive reading has been linked to improvement in general knowledge, vocabulary, spelling, fluency, and reading comprehension (Cunningham & Stanovich, 2001; Krashen, 2004). Also, the amount of reading students do is positively correlated with word identification skills, academic achievement, comprehension, reading fluency, and writing (Cunningham & Allington, 2010; Guthrie, Wigfield, Metsala, & Cox, 2004). Finally, increasing the time spent reading independently has been shown to be an effective way to reduce the gap between high- and low-achieving readers (Allington, 2012; Krashen, 2004).

The first part of this chapter describes strategies for promoting voluntary reading with struggling readers. The chapter ends with a description of four instructional approaches that have been shown to be effective in working with struggling readers in multilevel settings.

Source: Thinkstock/Stockbyte.

STRATEGIES FOR PROMOTING VOLUNTARY READING

Voluntary reading is the type of reading that students do on their own outside of school or class assignments. This section contains strategies for promoting this.

• **Help students fall in love with books.** Reading is a pleasurable act. That's why so many people do it. Your prime directive as a teacher of reading should be to help your students fall in love with reading. Once this occurs, much of your reading instruction takes care of itself.

• **Make good books readily available.** Students will read for pleasure if they have something pleasurable to read. In your classroom, you'll need to have an assortment of interesting and enjoyable books. These books should be of varying levels (two to six reading levels above and below grade level), both narrative and expository, and encompassing a wide range of genre, types, and subjects.

• **Include high/low and high/very-low books.** High/low and high/very-low books are described in Chapter 12. These should be included in school and classroom libraries and also used as part of instruction with struggling readers.

• **Practice reading every day.** Just as one practices a musical instrument or an athletic skill, students need daily reading practice if they are to improve their reading skills. Students in the primary grades generally need a minimum of 15 minutes of independent reading practice each day (although more is always better). Students in the intermediate grades generally need a minimum of 20 minutes of independent reading practice every day. Students in high school generally need a minimum of 30 minutes of independent reading practice every day. These times are merely suggestions to give you a sense of where to start. It may take time initially to develop the reading stamina necessary to read for this long, especially if students haven't had experience with independent reading.

Reading practice should occur every day (Allington, 2012). It shouldn't be bumped or impinged upon by other activities or special events. Also, reading practice should be used just for reading. It shouldn't be used to catch up on other work, to test, to conference, to grade, to study, to do homework, or to do anything other than read and enjoy books. Also, daily reading practice should reflect the types of reading that adults do in the real world when we read for pleasure. Thus, students should be able to choose the books they will read and they should be able to read independently without the threat of comprehension worksheets, book reports, or quizzes. There are other times and places to assess comprehension.

• **Read to students.** Having an ongoing book that you read out loud to your students is a simple yet effective way to draw them into books. It also provides rich opportunities for incidental learning related to events, concepts, and vocabulary. Even five to ten minutes a day will expose your students to a variety of authors, characters, new vocabulary, genre, and concepts. It can also be effective in helping students settle down so that they're able to concentrate after a recess or at the beginning of a reading class.

• **Validate light reading.** When you and I go into a library or bookstore we don't look for books that will challenge us. We look for books that we'll enjoy. Allow students the same privileges we enjoy. Remember, for reading practice, students should be reading books at their independent reading level or below. For voluntary reading, there is no such thing as a book that's "too easy."

• **Assign reading homework**. Wide reading exposes students to more words, increases word recognition and reading fluency, facilitates word learning, and helps to expand students' knowledge base (Krashen, 2004). To facilitate these things, an effective homework assignment is to simply ask students to find a good book and enjoy it for 10 to 15 minutes every night. Create reading logs (see Figure 9.1) for students to document their progress here. These logs can be traditional paper or embedded into a website. If you wish to assign grades, give students points for completion and maintenance of their reading logs.

• **Use book talks.** A book talk is where a student simply tells the class about a book he or she has read and enjoyed. You'll need to teach students how to do a book talk initially by modeling this for them.

Figure 9.1   Reading Homework Assignment Log

Book	Date	Time	Pages	Enjoyment Level
The Lightning Thief	March 12	7:00–7:20 p.m.	338–345	8
The Lightning Thief	March 13	7:05–7:25 p.m.	346–360	10
Number the Stars	March 14	7:00–7:30 p.m.	1–20	8

Enjoyment Level Key:

10 = very high enjoyment; 5 = average enjoyment; 1 = very low enjoyment

Book talks are very informal, lasting anywhere from 15 seconds to no more than two minutes. It's a short commercial for a particular book where students describe a book they've read and tell why they liked it. Hearing other students describe good books is an excellent way to get students interested in reading and gives them ideas for what they might like to read next.

It works best to schedule no more than two or three book talks a day. Keep a calendar for students to use to sign up. In the upper levels, if you want to make this a part of students' grade, give them the full points simply for doing them. Do not make them performance oriented. Keep in mind that these are NOT oral book reports. They're also not quizzes designed to see if students have read or comprehend the book. They should look very much like the conversations you might have with friends if you were telling them about a great book you had read.

• **Have students create book posters.** A book poster is like a movie posters except for books. Encourage students to create book posters for books they like.

• **Use book critiques.** Conversation of any kind related to books creates an awareness of reading and invites students to analyze text at deeper levels. One simple way to do this is to have students assume the role of a book critic (see Chapter 13). At the emergent and beginning levels, you can do this with ribbon ratings. After reading a book, students decide if it's a blue, red, or yellow ribbon book. A blue ribbon is outstanding, a red ribbon is okay, and a yellow ribbon is a stinker. Paper plates can be used here to create some simple ribbons. Students write the name of the book in the center along with their name. They can also draw a picture or write comments about the book. Put these up on a bulletin board or on a wall where they can be easily seen. The books that are rated highly become commercials for other students. When students disagree with a rating, the discussion that ensues invites higher levels of thinking and analysis.

• **Create a recommended book list.** There are many organizations that publish lists of children and young-adult books that have been recommended by teachers, students, and librarians (see Figure 9.2). These lists can be used to give you and your students a sense of what others have found to be good books. You can also help your students create their own top 10 (or 20) book lists. These lists should be always evolving.

Figure 9.2   Websites for Interesting or Important Book Lists

• National Education Association (NEA) teachers' top 100 books for children:

   http://www.nea.org/readacross/resources/catalist.html

• International Reading Association's (IRA) book choice list:

   http://www.reading.org/resources/tools/choices.html

• National Education Association's (NEA) kids' top 100 books:

   http://www.nea.org/readacross/resources/kidsbooks.html

• **Trust students to read**. Imagine how our reading habits would change if we had to take a quiz or fill out a comprehension worksheet every time we read in order to see if we read the book. You do not have to hold students accountable for everything they read.

• **Allow student choice**. Imagine how our reading habits would change if, upon entering a library or bookstore, we were told which books we had to read or buy. Just like adults, our students should be able to choose their reading material. However, choice does not have to mean total choice all the time. To the greatest degree possible, allow students to choose their reading material. Choice is a powerful motivator and is an important factor in reading development (Allington, 2012). Choice can also include when to read, how to read, and where they read. Choice might also include allowing students to make choices about how they might respond to a book. For example,

they might wish to make an entry in a reading log, engage in a structured conversation, be part of a literature circle or book club, create a
book poster or some other art project, or make an online commercial
for their book.

• **Allow students to stop reading books that they do not find
enjoyable**. You and I are able to stop reading books that we do not
find enjoyable. Give your students this same opportunity. There are
plenty of good books to read. There is no need for students to waste
time reading books they do not find to be enjoyable

• **Create opportunities for conversation and social interactions
around books**.

INSTRUCTIONAL APPROACHES

This section describes four instructional approaches that work especially well in meeting the needs of all students in multilevel settings.

Language Experience Approach

The language experience approach (LEA) is an important part of
reading instruction for emergent and beginning readers as well as students with significant reading difficulties. Here students describe an
experience while the teacher writes down what they say. Students then
practice reading using words and concepts within their experience.
This can be done individually with students in a tutoring session. It can
also be done in large or small groups with an interactive whiteboard,
overhead projector, a large sheet of paper, or any other writing space in
which students can see the words and sentences as you write them.

Directions for doing LEA: First ask students, "What do you want
to say about . . . " and write down what they say. For example, if your
class took a field trip to the zoo, you would say, "Boys and girls, what
should we say about our trip to the zoo yesterday?" A student might
say something like, "We went on a bus and it was a long trip and it
was really, really fun." Often you'll need to paraphrase or break up
their long sentences into two or three short sentences to make it more
likely for students to be successful. You might say something like,
"We went on the bus. It was a long trip." Then ask, "What else do you
want to say?"

Next, use ScORe to read through the entry the first time. Then,
have the student reread until fluency is achieved. Finally, you can

reinforce letter sounds or patterns at the end by asking students to identify and read aloud words that contain specific letters or letter patterns.

Figure 9.3 contains an example of an LEA done with an individual student (Pat). Here the teacher and Pat were able to make personal connections as well as practice reading. A Word document was created and saved with the date of the entry posted on top. Pat could then practice rereading past entries. Also, activities and minilessons were designed using students' own writing. This made them much more impactful. The teacher created books to practice reading by collecting these LEA stories over time.

Figure 9.3   An Example of LEA Writing in a Student's Journal

---

Pat's Journal

Tuesday, December 3. What do you want to tell us today? *(Minimum of 5 sentences in paragraph form.)*

I went to my grandma's house for Thanksgiving. My cousin couldn't come because he is in college. We had turkey and stuffing and mashed potatoes. I went to my cousin's friend's house before we ate. It was great.

Self-Selected or Reading Workshop Approach

The self-selected approach meets the needs of all readers within a single instruction setting and it offers both choice and challenge. While this instructional approach may seem more complicated at the outset, once you understand the basic principles, reading workshop is actually a much simpler and more effective way to teach reading. This is because students are able to enjoy good books, and you are able to teach exactly what students need. I'll provide the basics here.

• **Independent Reading.** Reading and enjoying good books is at the heart of reading workshop. Here students (and often the teacher) read books that they've selected. The duration here can be from 10 minutes to 90 minutes.

What if students don't read? Find good books, and they will read. If the choice is between sitting and doing nothing and reading a good book, students always choose reading a book. It may not happen the first day, but if you have good books at their independent level and below, students will eventually read.

How do you know if students are reading? Watch them. Look at their eyeballs. Watch them turn the pages. See on which pages or pictures they seem to linger. Ask them questions about what they're reading. These things all provide important information about your students as readers.

How do you know if students comprehend what they read? There are times and places to formally assess comprehension. You do not have to formally assess everything students read. Trust them to read and enjoy good books. However, by examining their reading logs (below), conducting reading conferences (below), and by listening to their conversations around books you will know if and to what degree students comprehend what they read.

• **Minilessons.** Direct, explicit, and systematic instruction is used to teach word identification skills and other reading strategies. These are taught in large group, small group, and individually using mini-lessons that last anywhere from 2 to 10 minutes. A scope and sequence chart can be used to give you a sense of what to teach initially (see Chapter 10); however, your students are the best scope and sequence chart there is. Based on your observation of students engaged in authentic reading, you'll see exactly what skills need to be taught and to whom.

• **Reading Log/Journal.** A reading log or journal is an empty notebook or word document that students use to respond to the books that they are reading. It's also used for writing practice, minilessons, and pre- and post-reading activities. A notebook or word document is far less expensive and more utilitarian than consumable workbooks. Reading logs also enable you to differentiate instruction, assignments, and activities to meet the different needs, ability levels, and interests of your students.

• **Conferences.** Conferences are opportunities for teachers to listen to students read, to ask questions, and to take notes. Your notes become the basis for future minilessons. They can be done with students individually or in small groups. An individual conference takes between five and ten minutes. Doing a conference with three students a day enables you to touch base with each of your students every two or three weeks. It's also a very direct and authentic form of assessment.

• **Portfolio Assessment.** Portfolio assessment is often used with reading workshop. Included here could be things such as the following: books read, fluency scores, samples from student reading logs, checklists, your notes from student conferences, and students' reflections and observations of their reading, along with more traditional items such as scores on end-of-unit tests. Students could also document and create their own portfolio submissions (see Figure 9.4).

Figure 9.4 Ideas for Student Portfolio Submissions

Monthly Reading Description Chart

Books Read	Date Completed
1.	1.
2.	2.
3.	3.

Interesting topics, subjects, or ideas read about:

1.

2.

3.

Genre or Types of Books Read

__ fantasy	__ science fiction	__ fantasy
__ picture book	__ historical fiction	__ historical
__ realistic fiction	__ fairy tales	__ information book
__ detective/mystery	__ adventure	
	__ horror/scary	__ biography
		__ other

Describe an interesting character from a book you've read:

Number of book talks _____

Number of book reviews _____

(Continued)

(Continued)

What books or kinds of books would you like to read next month?

What are your reading goals for next month?

What kinds of things do you like to read?

What did you do well this month?

What do you do if you don't know a word?

What (if anything) seems to give you trouble when reading?

What can your teacher do to help you become a better reader?

Skills I use to help me comprehend information books:

__ Take notes	__ Dot and notes	__ Article reread
__ Paragraph reread	__ Read and pause	__ Other (describe below) _____
__ 3 × 5 card	__ Preview/overview	_____

Basal-Reading Workshop Approach

A basal-reading series is a teaching tool. Like any tool, its effectiveness is dependent on how it's used. An ineffective way to use a basal-reading series is to do every worksheet, activity, and assignment exactly as described and in the prescribed order. Why? This assumes that one type of instruction fits all students and teachers. Keep in mind that the publishers don't know your students, their interests, their specific strengths, or the specific areas with which they need extra help. Neither do they know you, your teaching style, your pedagogical repertoire, or your teaching philosophy.

An effective way to use a basal-reading series is to adopt and flexibly adapt only those parts of it that you deem appropriate for your students. This can be done using a basal-reading workshop approach. Below are some of the key elements of this approach.

• **Use of Basal Reader as an Anthology.** Just like the reading workshop above, the key element of the basal-reading workshop is students reading books that they've selected. The basal here is used as an anthology or a collection of stories for students to read. Instead of purchasing a very expensive hardcover book for each student in your class, you would only need to purchase five or six total copies. (The money saved here could be used to buy real books that students enjoy.) These basal readers are housed in the classroom library or put on a front table. Students are allowed to select the stories that they wish to read. If you want to expose students to a certain type of genre, select one or two mandatory stories for students to read each week.

• **Basal-Based Minilessons.** Often administrators insist teachers teach straight from the basal in order to "cover" all the necessary skills. From a literacy learning perspective, this makes little sense. However, if you wish to appease administrators, you can still teach the skills outlined in the basal workbooks. Often these skills can be taught more effectively outside of the commercially prepared workbook using shared reading, guided reading, daily oral language, or minilessons as part of a language experience activity. If you do use worksheets and workbooks, I recommend that you create scaffolded instruction in large-group or small-group settings, working on them together so that conversation and cognitive modeling can be part of the learning process. Worksheets and workbooks are teaching tools to enhance learning; however, the goal is not for students to be able to complete worksheets but to be able to create meaning with print.

• **End-of-Unit Tests.** Most basal programs include both end-of-unit tests and remedial tests. Use the remedial tests for short minilessons. Here you'll be teaching test-taking strategies as well as reinforcing the skills taught. When students are ready, use the end-of-unit tests to document their progress. I would encourage you to use your professional knowledge and expertise to make decisions as to which of the skills covered in a basal are necessary for enhancing students ability to create meaning with print. Include only the necessary elements in your instruction and assessment.

The Four Blocks™ Approach

The Four Blocks™ approach to literacy instruction recognizes that all students can learn to read and write, but they do not all learn the same way (Cunningham, Hall, & Defee, 1998). Thus, instruction must support different learning styles. It incorporates four types of instruction (blocks) every day: Guided Reading, Writing, Working With Words, and Self-Selected Reading. Four Blocks™ is designed for use in an inclusive general education setting, but can also be used in a resource room. It has also been successfully adopted for use with struggling readers by Karen Erickson and David Koppenhaver (2007).

There are two guiding principles: First, all children can learn to read and write without being labeled and ability grouped. Second, students must be exposed to each block every day. Each block should run at least 30 to 40 minutes. A brief description of each block is provided below.

• **Guided Reading.** Instruction usually begins with the Guided Reading block. Here the teacher chooses the material for students to read and then guides them in the use of reading strategies or skills. A variety of formats could be used including a scaffolded reading experience (SRE) lesson, guided reading lesson, or shared reading lesson format (see Chapter 5). With younger students, choral reading and echo reading can be used. With older students, partner reading, book clubs, group reads, or even silent reading can be used as long as there are supports in place to enable readers of all ability levels to have easy access to the text. Typical supports include outlines or audio recordings.

• **Writing.** During the Writing block a structure is created to enable all students to write on topics of their own choice and at their own pace. (Choice is a powerful motivator in any literacy endeavor.) It usually begins with a whole-class minilesson related to some aspect of writing, lasting from two to eight minutes. Students then work on their own writing projects which may be in any of five stages (prewriting, drafting, editing, revising, or sharing), and at their own pace. Other elements included are individual- and group-writing conferences, individual- and small-group minilessons, editing tables, students reading and responding to the writing of others, illustrating, book publishing, website development, author's chair, and portfolio assessment. For struggling writers, speech-to-text software (it writes what you say) and text-to-speech software (it reads back what you have written) can be effective.

• **Working With Words.** Working With Words involves work with spelling, sight words, phonics, and word identification skills (cloze, analogy, morphemic analysis, word order, phonics, and sight words). Any of the strategies described in Chapter 10 and Chapter 11 can be used here.

• **Self-Selected Reading**. Self-Selected Reading is run very much like reading workshop (see above). The same elements apply except the minilesson. Minilessons would be included either in Guided Reading or Working with Words blocks.

Last Word

This chapter described the importance of voluntary reading. The following strategies were described for promoting voluntary reading:

- Help students fall in love with books.
- Make good books readily available.
- Include high/low and high/very-low books.
- Use student-written books.
- Use daily-reading practice.
- Read to students.
- Validate light reading.
- Assign reading as homework.
- Use book talks, book posters, and book critiques
- Create a recommended book lists.
- Trust students to read.
- Allow student choice, including the choice to stop reading books.
- Create opportunities for conversation and social interactions around books.

This chapter described four instructional approaches that work well in meeting the needs of all students in multilevel settings: (a) the language experience approach, (b) self-select or reading-workshop approach, (c) basal-reading workshop approach, and (d) the Four Blocks™ approach.

10

Phonics

The goal with phonics activities is to strengthen neural pathways so that students can process letters and words quickly.

Fawnix

Phonics is the ability to associate sounds with letters or letter patterns. Phonics is one of six ways to identify individual words as we read. The other five are the following: (a) analogy [word families], (b) morphemic awareness [prefix, suffix, affix, root], (c) context clues [semantics], (d) syntax [word order], and (e) sight words. (These will be described in more detail in the next chapter.) Phonics instruction is very important, but it should never be taught as the sole component in any reading program (Erickson, Hanser, Hatch, & Sanders, 2009; McCormick & Zutell, 2011; National Institute for Child Health and Development, 2000). Reading instruction that is effective utilizes all six word identification skills.

Tips for Developing Phonetic Cueing Systems

Following are three tips for helping to develop students' phonetic cueing system.

1. **Teach the minimum amount of phonics necessary**. The goal of any type of reading instruction is to help children create meaning with text. If children seem to be doing this without too much trouble, leave them alone.

2. **Instruction should be explicit, short, and briskly paced**. Children do not learn phonics as much as they gradually develop the ability to use this cueing system. Explicit-phonics instruction is necessary, but it should be brief and allow plenty of opportunities to practice. Nancie Atwell suggests that 20% to 30% of reading class be used for skills instruction (Atwell, 1998). This means that 70% to 80% of the time devoted to reading instruction should be used for reading practice. Again, the goal of reading is to be able create meaning with text, not to do phonics activities or complete worksheets.

3. **Do not focus on phonics to the exclusion of the other cueing systems**. Reading instruction should always be balanced (National Institute for Child Health and Development, 2000). It should develop students' ability to use the phonetic cueing system and at the same time strengthen the semantic and syntactic cueing systems. (The next chapter will describe these.)

Systematic Phonics Instruction

Phonics instruction should be systematic (Erickson, Hanser, Hatch, & Sanders, 2009; Houston, Al Otaiba, & Torgesen, 2006). However, systematic phonics instruction does not mean that you have to follow a rigid plan where all students are taught the same skills in the same way and in the same, prescribed order. Instead, systematic means that you have some sort of plan for addressing common letter-sound associations such as consonants, consonant blends, vowels, and word families. You can use a basic scope and sequence chart to give you a sense of what skills to teach (see Figure 10.1); however, the best scope and sequence chart is your students. Watch and listen to them as they read. See what skills they need and teach them these skills explicitly.

In general, it is best to start with letter sounds focusing on beginning consonants and vowel sounds. Gradually move into beginning consonant blends and then the common word families. As far as vowel diagraphs, diphthongs, the schwa sound, and r-controlled vowel sounds go, they are too inconsistent and infrequent to spend a lot of time with them. I will say this again, skillful readers use

Figure 10.1 Common Scope and Sequence Chart

Consonants	Vowel Digraph Syllables
(all)	ee (feet), ea (each), oo (boot), ai (bait), ay (stay), oa (boat), ou (out), ow (cow), aw (saw), au (taught), oy (boy), oi (oil)
Short Vowels	**Endings**
a, i, o, u, e	silent e (house), es, ed, er, ing, ful, n't
Long Vowels	**r-Controlled Vowels**
A, I, O, U, E, Y	ar, ear, er, ir, ur, or (word), ar (warm)
Consonant Blends (front)	**Soft c and g**
sl, st, sp, sn, sc, sw, sk, sm, br, cr, dr, fr, pr, tr, gr, scr, spr, str, cl, fl, pl, bl, gl, spl, tw	c (ice), g (gnaw), gh (through), g (manage), g (dg—bridge)
Consonant Blends (end)	**Long Vowel With Magic /e/ Ending**
st, sk, sp, nd, nt, lt, lk, lf, ld, lp, lm, lb, lc, mp, ct, ft, pt	lake, bike, note, Pete, mute
Consonant Digraphs and Trigraphs	**More Long Vowels**
sh, ch, tch, th (unvoiced), wh, ck	ie (chief), ei (seize), ey (key), y (fly), ie (pie), igh (sigh), oe (toe), ou (soul), old (gold), oll (roll), olt (bolt), ue (true), ew (new), ui (fruit), eigh (eight), ei (vein), ey (hey)
Double Consonants at End	
ff, ss, ll, bb, gg, dd, nn, tt, zz, qu, xx	**Silent Letters and Advanced**
ng and nk Patterns	sc (scent), wr (wrap), kn (knee), gn (gnaw), ign (sign), gh (taught), ought (thought), ph (phone), tion (action), sion (mansion), sion (vision), ci (special), ti (patient), ture (picture)
ing, ang, ength, ong, ung, ink, ank, unk, onk	

minimal-letter cues when identifying words. It makes sense then that phonics instruction be as minimal as possible.

In Chapter 1, we saw how relatively unimportant vowels are. Based on this and on what we know about how the brain creates meaning with print, eye movement research, cognitive processing, and examining how efficient readers identify words, I would recommend limiting instruction to those reading subskills in Figure 10.2.

(I know there will be varying thoughts on this.) The phonics checklist in the Appendix at the end of this chapter (page 134) can be used to record when you teach each subskill. You can also create an individual phonics checklist for each student in your class to record when he or she has mastered each reading subskill. By listening to three or four students read each day, you will be able to document each student's mastery of these reading subskills every two weeks.

Figure 10.2   Recommended Reading Subskills Chart

Consonants

(all)

Short Vowels

a, i, o, u, e

Long Vowels

A, I, O, U, E, Y

Consonant Blends (Beginning)

sl, st, sp, sn, sc, sw, sk, sm, br, cr, dr, fr, pr, tr, gr, scr, spr, str, cl, fl, pl, bl, gl, spl, tw

Sight Words

Zeno, Dolch, Fry, or MFW

Word Families

38 most common phonograms

Types of Phonics Instruction

There are two general types of phonics instruction. I recommend that both be used in the teaching of phonics.

• **Synthetic Phonics Instruction.** *Synthetic phonics instruction* teaches students to identify letter sounds first and then to synthesize or put these sounds together to create words. This is the approach taken by traditional skills-based programs. It is sometimes called the part-to-whole approach. Here students first learn to target word parts or letter sounds using direct instruction. Then, students are given reading material that emphasizes the letter sound in order to reinforce it.

• **Analytic Phonics Instruction.** *Analytic phonics instruction* includes any strategy that teaches students to analyze the sounds within words they already know. It starts at the level of the whole word, ideally found within the context of a sentence and then moves to the individual parts. That is, students are taught to look for common word parts or families that they recognize within words. This is sometimes referred to as the whole-to-part approach. Explicit phonics instruction is used, but it is embedded within the texts students are reading to the greatest degree possible.

Two examples of strategies that reflect an analytic approach are described here:

Example 1. Mr. Hill puts the sentences in Figure 10.3 on a interactive whiteboard so that his whole class can see them. Together, the class reads them out loud twice, using choral reading as Mr. Hill points to each word. After reading, Mr. Hill tells the class that he is looking for words that have the "buh" sound. He asks volunteers to use the pointer to find the "buh" words. He then tells students that the letter /b/ makes the "buh" sound. He shows them many examples on the interactive whiteboard, using words and pictures of words that begin with the /b/ sound. Students practice by reading through a list of more words and pictures that also start with the /b/ sound. Later on, students create a predictable writing chart, "Things That Are Big" (Figure 10.4).

Figure 10.3   Example of an Analytic Approach

Billy rode to school today on the bus. He likes to play baseball. He also loves biting big apples.

Figure 10.4   Predictable Writing Chart

Things That Are Big

A bus is big.
A tree is big.
A cloud is big.
A school is big.

Example 2. Ms. Tate is working individually with Bob, a fifth-grade student. She asks Bob what he did over the weekend. As Bob tells her, she writes what he says on the computer. (This is the language experience approach described in Chapter 9.) After they have finished writing, she reads it through once with Bob, and then Bob reads it through until he can read it fluently. Then, Ms. Tate asks him to find examples of specific target words. "There's a word that ends with the 'st' sound. There's a word with a short *a* vowel in the second line." Finally, she has him take apart some of the larger words, identifying and sounding out each recognizable part.

14 STRATEGIES

Described below are 14 strategies for developing students' phonetic cueing system. There is nothing new or magical about these: adopt and adapt. Use the ones that seem most effective for you and your students.

1. **Teaching Basic Letter-Sound Association**. Basic phonics instruction looks like this: "This is the letter /b/, it makes the 'buh' sound. Here are examples of words that have the 'buh' sound." This type of explicit instruction is necessary, but it should be kept brief. There are an abundance of good phonics websites, games, and activities on the Internet that can be used to reinforce your initial instruction; however, these should not take the place of your explicit instruction. There are also apps and games for your IPads or other tablets. Do not become enamored with any one program or approach, however. Some parts of some programs may work best for some students some of the time, but no parts of any program work best for all students at any time.

2. **Pairs and Small-Group Worksheets**. Worksheets are a tool and like any tool, their effectiveness is determined by how they are used. Worksheets are often most effective as learning tools when students work in pairs or even in small groups to complete them. The conversation that takes place between students enhances learning. Also, worksheets can be used during skills instruction as a form of guided practice or to reinforce skills that have already been taught.

3. **The Elements of Effective-Skills Instruction.** Phonics instruction should be brief and briskly paced. Use the elements of effective skills instruction found in Figure 10.5 (Johnson, 2009). Do not expect

mastery in a single lesson. With any reading subskill, mastery comes over time through repeated practice and exposure.

Figure 10.5   Johnson Skills Lesson-Plan Format

Skills Lesson-Plan Format for Teaching Phonics Skills*

Based on the elements of effective skills instruction.

I. **Goal.** Students will learn about [insert phonetic element here].

II. **Input**

1. **Identification of Procedural Components.** Introduce the target letter sound or letter-sound pattern with the corresponding sound.

2. **Direct Instruction and Modeling.** Demonstrate the target letter sound in the context of a word. Point to the letter. Use many examples. If possible, include pictures with the words. Include nonexamples as well.

3. **Guided Practice (Scaffolded Instruction).** Guide students in their development of the target skill. This can also be used as a type of formative assessment. Activities here are all done under teacher supervision. Examples of guided practice for a phonics lesson include the following: students identify examples of the target letter sound, students distinguish between examples and nonexamples of the target letter sound, students complete a worksheet together in a large group, or students work with a partner to complete a worksheet.

III. **Activity**

4. **Independent Practice.** Provide independent practice of the skill students have just learned. The goal here is to reinforce learning (not measurement or evaluation). Students should complete this with 95–100% success ratios. Examples of independent practice for phonics include the following: worksheets done individually, with a partner, or in small group; writing prompts that get students using the target letter sound; activities or games that reinforce the letter sound; independent writing; or independent reading.

4. **Treasure Hunt.** After introducing a letter sound, ask students to find similar letter sounds in texts they have already read. Here students review the story and write the words they find in the reading log or data retrieval chart (see Figure 10.6). Students can work individually, in pairs, or in small groups.

5. **Personal Dictionary.** Students create a personal dictionary using words with target letter sounds. If you use a notebook, ask students to draw a picture or symbol next to each word to help them remember it. If you use a computer, help them find pictures to go with their words. Have students practice their words frequently by reading them to a partner. For example, "With your partner, let's practice our short /a/ words today." You can also create activities that have students using target words. Example: "Select a word from your short /a/ page. Create a silly sentence (in writing or orally) using that word."

Figure 10.6 Data Retrieval Chart for Treasure Hunts

Short a	Short u

6. **Word Sorts.** Create cards with words based on the 38 phonograms and most frequent words (MFW) in the Appendix at the end of this chapter (page 134). Give students 8 to 20 cards. Ask them to create groups based on letter patterns. Encourage them to create their own letter groups.

7. **Concentration.** This game gets students analyzing words and letter sounds in order to reinforce their phonetic knowledge. Write the MFW and phonogram words on 3 × 5 cards. Include two words that represent specific letter sounds. (For example, two short /a/ words or two /ig/ words.) Turn these upside down. Students turn over cards to find pairs or words that include the same vowel sounds. You can play this game focusing on vowel sounds, consonants, blends, or phonograms.

8. **Letter Bodies.** This works best for grades preK–2. To get students physically involved, have them create the letter with their arms or their bodies. For example, in teaching the short /a/ sound, you would ask students to make their bodies into the shape of a short /a/ when they hear you say a short /a/ word (you will have to demonstrate this). This can be done with consonants as well as vowel sounds. Do two or three letter sounds at a time. Eventually, you can create dances based on letter sounds. Using music or a rhythm, call out letter sounds or words. You can extend this further by playing Simon Says using letter bodies. Another game is to have students spell a word using letter bodies, and see if the class can guess the word.

9. **Word Walls.** A word wall is composed of groups of words posted on a wall or bulletin board in some form (see Figure 10.7). These words are groups by the letter sounds you are trying to reinforce. (They can also be grouped by concept.) You can use word walls in a variety of ways. For example, ask simple riddles: "I'm thinking of a short /a/ word. It is something you do when you are tired." Use them as writing or speaking prompts. Example: "We're looking at a long /A/ word: pain. Describe a time when you felt pain."

Figure 10.7 Example of a Word Wall

Short a	Long A	b	d
ant	name	ball	dog
nap	ape	bean	dig
tab	made	bake	dip
fast	paste	bark	doll
bat	nail	bun	dot

10. **The Riddle Game.** This strategy is similar to word building, which will be described in more detail in the next chapter. Here students are given a phonogram such as /ap/ and five to eight letters or blends. They are asked to add a letter or blend to the front to answer a riddle (see Figure 10.8). Example: "I have the /ap/ family. If I am cold I want this on my head. What beginning sound do I need to add?" Finally, reinforce this by saying "'c' plus 'ap' is cap," and then write the entire word *cap* on the board or piece of paper. At the end read through the entire list of words until students can read them fluently. You can extend the game by asking students to create their own riddles for the class.

Figure 10.8 The Riddle Game for Beginning Sounds

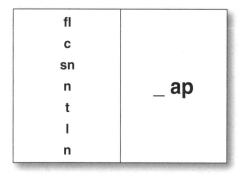

11. **Wordo.** Wordo is a variation of Bingo. Create a list of words that focus on two or three target phonograms or letter sounds. Give students an empty Wordo card (Figure 10.9). As you write and say the words on the board, students write the word anywhere on their Wordo card. Each word should also be

written on a 3 × 5 card. Students are then given chips or markers of some kind. Randomly pick a card, say the target letter sound, then say the whole word. Do not show the word yet. Ask students to put a marker over a similar word. Then show the word and give students a chance to make changes. Just like in bingo, a row in any direction creates a winner. For young students, use a 4 × 4 word card or a 3 × 3 can card (I can read). You can play several times using the same chart.

Figure 10.9   Variations of the Wordo Card

Wordo Card

w	o	r	d	o

Word Card

w	o	r	d

Can Card

c	a	n

12. **Scaffolded Writing.** One of the best ways to teach and reinforce phonics as well as spelling patterns is scaffolded writing. As the name implies, here you provide a scaffold for students by helping them hear and identify letters as they are writing. That is, you sound out the parts of the word as the student is writing. For example, Mr. Bell is working individually with Mary, a second-grade student. He asks her what she wants to write about today. She says, "It's cold today." Mr. Bell repeats, "It is cold today." He repeats the sentence slowly. Then he repeats each word as she is writing so she can hear the sounds within each word as she writes.

With all scaffolded activities the goal is to enable students to be as independent as possible without frustrating them. To avoid the frustration of finding keys, point to the area where the target key is on the keyboard. After the first word is spelled, repeat the entire sentence and go to the next word. Do this for all the words in the sentence. With students who have severe reading and writing difficulties, your initial goal should be to write one or two sentences at most.

13. **Dictated Sentences Using Temporary Spelling.** Dictated sentences are used to reinforce letter sounds or phonograms. Here you create one to three short sentences for the student to write. Include one word with the letter or phonogram you wish to reinforce. Use sight words where appropriate. Sentences should be between three and five words. With struggling readers and writers, start with two sentences.

As the student is writing, repeat each word of the sentence, but do not help with spelling at this phase. Instead, tell the student to use one or two letters to hold the idea. When the sentence is completed, ask the student to identify words that don't look right. Students are usually able to find the misspelled words. Then, put a line through the misspelled word and write the correct spelling on top. Have the student write the correct spelling on the bottom. Skip a line and go to the next sentence. If you're using a keyboard, help the student use spellcheck. Finally, when you have completed all sentences, ask the student to reread them until they can be read fluently.

14. **Text-to-Speech Software.** Writing is a powerful way to reinforce letter-sound patterns within the context of an authentic literacy activity. Text-to-speech writing software programs make the individual letter sound as students press the keys. When students complete a word, it reads back the word. Students are also able to have the program reread a sentence or paragraph that has been composed.

Last Word

This chapter described tips for developing students' phonetic cueing system, an alternative way to think about systematic phonics instruction, and synthetic and analytic phonics instruction. The following strategies were also described for developing students' phonetic cueing system:

- Basic letter-sound association
- Pairs and small group worksheets
- Elements of effective skills instruction
- Treasure hunt
- Personal dictionary
- Word sorts
- Concentration
- Letter bodies
- Word walls
- Riddle game
- Wordo
- Scaffolded writing
- Sentence dictation using temporary spelling
- Text-to-speech software

Keep in mind that the goal with phonics activities is to strengthen neural pathways so that students can process letters and words quickly. Phonics should be just part of your total-reading program. Make sure you give equal attention to activities that develop the other two cueing systems (see Chapter 11).

APPENDIX: PHONICS CHECKLIST

Check off (or date) when you observe students using and mastering the phonics skills and sight words below.

Consonants				
___ B	___ H	___ M	___ R	___ W
___ C	___ J	___ N	___ S	___ X
___ F	___ K	___ P	___ T	___ Z
___ G	___ L	___ Q	___ V	

Short Vowel Sounds				
___ a	___ e	___ i	___ o	___ u

Long Vowel Sounds					
___ A	___ E	___ I	___ O	___ U	___ Y

Beginning Blends					
___ sl	___ sc	___ br	___ pr	___ spr	___ bl
___ st	___ sw	___ cr	___ tr	___ cl	___ gl
___ sp	___ sk	___ dr	___ gr	___ fl	___ spl
___ sn	___ sm	___ fr	___ scr	___ pl	___ tw

38 Most Common Phonograms							
___ ay	___ ag	___ ot	___ ain	___ op	___ ow	___ ob	___ ight
___ ill	___ ack	___ ing	___ eed	___ in	___ ew	___ ock	___ im
___ ip	___ ank	___ ap	___ y	___ an	___ ore	___ ake	___ uck
___ at	___ ick	___ unk	___ out	___ est	___ ed	___ ine	___ um
___ am	___ ell	___ all	___ ug	___ ink	___ ab		

Fry 100 Most Frequent Words

___ the	___ at	___ there	___ some	___ my
___ of	___ be	___ use	___ her	___ than
___ and	___ this	___ an	___ would	___ first
___ a	___ have	___ each	___ make	___ water
___ to	___ from	___ which	___ like	___ been
___ in	___ or	___ she	___ him	___ call
___ is	___ one	___ do	___ into	___ who
___ you	___ had	___ how	___ time	___ oil
___ that	___ by	___ their	___ has	___ now
___ it	___ word	___ if	___ look	___ find
___ he	___ but	___ will	___ two	___ long
___ was	___ not	___ up	___ more	___ down
___ for	___ what	___ other	___ write	___ day
___ on	___ all	___ about	___ go	___ did
___ are	___ were	___ out	___ see	___ get
___ as	___ we	___ many	___ number	___ come
___ with	___ when	___ then	___ no	___ made
___ his	___ your	___ them	___ way	___ may
___ they	___ can	___ these	___ could	___ part
___ I	___ said	___ so	___ people	___ over

11

Strategies for Developing Word Identification Skills

We teach the process to develop the skill.

TERMS AND CONCEPTS
RELATED TO WORD IDENTIFICATION

This chapter describes a variety of strategies for developing and enhancing students' ability to identify words as they read. Let's first define some important terms.

Recognizing and Identifying Words

Word recognition refers to an instant or automatic recall of words without the use of any strategy, skill, or cognitive mechanism. Here your brain quickly and automatically processes words as you are reading. This is most likely what you're doing right now with the vast majority of words you're reading. You've encountered them many times before, and they're stored someplace in long-term memory. As you're reading, these words are accessible at various levels of ease or difficulty.

Word identification is a process or strategy used to figure out words that you don't automatically recognize. These words may be in long-term memory, but if so, the neural pathways aren't very well developed and thus, you don't recognize them instantly. Word identification also refers to strategies used when you encounter a new word (see Figure 11.1). For example, the first time I encountered the word *prosody* I needed to pause and reread the word. I looked at parts of the word to try to make sense of it. Then, I used the context of the sentence to try to figure out what it was. Finally, I used the dictionary function of my computer to look it up. The point is, I had to consciously employ a strategy.

Figure 11.1   Six Ways to Identify Words

1. Context clues (semantics)

2. Word order and grammar (syntax)

3. Word parts or analyzing words

4. Morphemic analysis (prefixes, suffixes, and root words)

5. Sight words

6. Phonics

Strategies and Skills

In educational terms, a *strategy* is a cognitive process that you consciously employ. A *skill* is a similar cognitive process; however, you engage in this automatically without thinking about it. Thus, we teach the process of identifying words as strategies for students to consciously employ when they encounter words they may not recognize. But the goal is always to develop the skill or to automatize the process so that students perceive words and word parts instantly while reading. We teach the process to develop the skill.

A Quick Review. Reading is creating meaning with print. Written words are used to help the reader create meaning. The brain uses three cueing systems to recognize these words as you read: semantics, syntax, and phonics. Of these three, phonics is the least efficient in terms of speed of processing and the amount of cognitive space necessary in short-term memory.

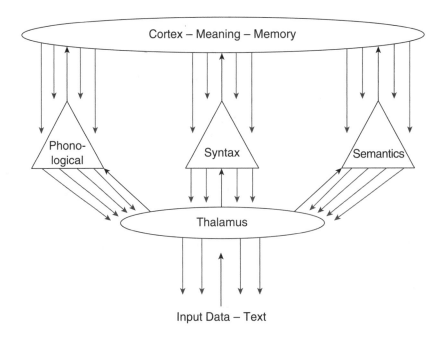

CONTEXT CLUES: THE SEMANTIC CUEING SYSTEM

As you read, your brain uses context and background knowledge to identify words, predict words, and go beyond the words to infer. This is the semantic-cueing system. Cloze and maze are the primary activities used to develop this cueing system.

Cloze

A *cloze* is a sentence with one word partially or completely covered or missing. For low-level readers, a first letter clue is usually included. Students must use the context of the sentence or paragraph to identify the missing or unknown word. Figure 11.2 shows examples of beginning-level cloze sentences.

Cloze activities can be done individually or with groups of students. Keep it fun and relatively brief. These are the steps:

1. Find or create cloze sentences. If possible, create sentences related to the students. You can also create sentences related to what students are reading or studying about. This produces a more meaningful reading experience and makes learning to read easier and more interesting.

Figure 11.2   Beginning-Level Cloze Sentences

These boys are **pl** _ _ _ _ _ soccer.
These boys are **playing** soccer.

It **l** _ _ _ _ like it is fun.
It **looks** like it is fun.

2. Present the sentence with the word covered up (or missing). If you are using a big book, chart, or paper for your sentences, cover the word with a sticky note.

    Sally likes to _ _ _ _ basketball.

3. Ask students, "What word would make sense in this sentence?" Write two or three of their ideas on the board or paper.

4. Uncover the first letter and ask, "Do you want to change your mind?"

5. Uncover the second letter and again ask, "Do you want to change your mind now?" By this time, most students will have figured out the word.

6. Reread the complete sentence. Ask students if the sentence makes sense.

Keep this activity simple. Its purpose is to develop students' ability to use context clues. Further practice and development of this skill comes from students' independent reading.

Maze

A *maze* is a sentence with two or three alternative words (see Figure 11.3). Students must select the word that makes the most sense in the sentence. Like cloze sentences, you can create a more meaningful experience by designing your own sentences around students' interests and experiences. Maze and cloze activities can also be used to reinforce words and concepts found in students' reading material or used in other curriculum areas. For example, you could design them to reinforce vocabulary and concepts from your science, social studies, health, math, or other subject areas. Finally, both maze and cloze can be used as pre-reading or post-reading activities.

Figure 11.3   Maze Sentences

Go [**bay—lay**] down.

Do you want to [**say—play**] cards?

The [**pot—pet**] is made of clay.

I will stay [**here—him**] today.

Which [**was—way**] did she go?

WORD ORDER AND GRAMMAR: THE SYNTACTIC-CUEING SYSTEM

As you read, your brain uses your knowledge of grammar, sentence structure, and word order to identify words, predict words, and make sense of the sentences you're reading. This is the syntactic-cueing system. Activities that focus on grammar, sentence structure, and word order are the primary activities used to develop this cueing system.

• **Writing, Writing, Writing.** Writing is good for almost everything pertaining to literacy including developing the syntactic-cueing system. Chapter 16 describes a variety of strategies that can be used here. Create opportunities for students to write on topics of their choice, reread and revise their own work, as well as listen and respond to the writing of other students.

• **Syntax Sentences**. Here, one to three sentences are presented to students that contain grammar or word-order errors. Students are called on to make the appropriate corrections. Like cloze and maze activities, create sentences to reinforce letter patterns, phonograms, sight words, or other areas of the curriculum, or use as pre- and post-reading activities.

- **Sentence Combining.** Students are given two or three sentences. They must combine them while retaining the initial meaning of both (see Figure 11.4).

Figure 11.4   Sentence Combining

Jill is strong.
Jill is a soccer player.

Andy is in the living room.
Andy spilled his milk.

- **Sentence Alteration.** Students are given a sentence and asked to say the same thing using different words or a different word order (see Figure 11.5).

Figure 11.5   Sentence Alteration

Please fill my glass.
Fill my glass please.
Will you fill my glass?
Can you fill my glass?
Put more in my glass.
My glass needs filling.
You should fill my glass.

- **Sentence Elaboration.** Students are given a sentence and asked to add to it to make it more interesting or different (see Figure 11.6). Encourage unique, creative, and humorous ideas here.

Again, since the focus is on grammar, sentence structure, and word order, all the activities above can be used to develop the syntactic-cueing system. They can also be used to reinforce letter patterns, phonograms, or sight words. As well, these can be used as pre- or post-reading activities by using sentences taken from or related to the text. With all of them, keep it simple and brief, using one to three sentences at a time.

Figure 11.6 Sentence Elaboration

> The woman cooked burgers on the grill.
>
> The old woman cooked burgers on the huge grill.
>
> The boy cooked tasty burgers on the rusty grill.
>
> The young man cooked hot dogs on the stove.

WORD PARTS

The activities in these next two sections (word parts and morphemic analysis) utilize the phonological-cueing system; however, instead of individual letters, the goal with these is to enable students to automatically recognize larger units within words.

Word Parts: A Strategy for Identifying Words

Word parts is a strategy in which students look for familiar parts within words to help them identify it. Teach it explicitly using the following steps:

1. Provide a sentence with a target word in it. If you are doing a guided reading lesson (see Chapter 5), select specific target words and sentences within the reading selection to use for the lesson.

2. Ask students if there are parts of the word that they recognize. For example, if the target word was *flipping* ask, "Is there any part of this word that you do recognize? Do you see any word parts or word families?" Then help students see the "fl" beginning blend, the "ip" word family, and the "ing" ending.

3. Ask students to use the word parts to construct a word or to make a guess.

4. Students should reread the sentence using the new word to see if it makes sense.

Word Parts: Pedagogical Strategies

Below are three simple strategies that can be used to help students develop the ability to recognize parts of words automatically as they read.

• **Analyzing Practice.** Present target words individually or in the context of a sentence (see Figure 11.7). Ask students to identify parts of words they recognize.

Figure 11.7   Analyzing Practice

preponderance	**can**tankerous
pre**pon**derance	can**tank**erous
prepon**der**ance	cantan**ker**ous
preponder**ance**	cantanker**ous**

• **The Big Word Bank.** After reading a story, ask students to identify and record interesting or important big words they encountered. Depending on the age, they should select one to three big words. Students create and record their words in a section of their reading journal or learning log called (appropriately) The Big Word Bank. Use these words for analyzing practice (above). These words can also be used for a variety of vocabulary, writing, grammar, and other word-identification activities.

• **Comparing Words.** Look for words, ideally found within students' current curriculum or reading material, that have similar parts. Have students compare the words to find the similar parts (see Figure 11.8).

Figure 11.8   Comparing Words

corres**pon**d	shr**ill**
s**pon**sor	inst**ill**
pond	sp**ill**way

Phonograms: Pedagogical Strategies

All the strategies in this section focus on phonograms or word families. The 38 most common phonograms are listed Figure 11.9

from most common to least (Fry, 1998). These can be used to help students identify approximately 654 one-syllable words. They can also be used to identify thousands of longer, multisyllable words. Use a systematic approach in teaching these (see Chapter 10). Again, the goal is to develop neural pathways so that students recognize these automatically as they are reading.

Figure 11.9   The 38 Most Common Phonograms

1. ay	8. ank	15. ail	22. in	29. ed	36. im
2. ill	9. ick	16. ain	23. an	30. ab	37. uck
3. ip	10. ell	17. eed	24. est	31. ob	38. um
4. at	11. ot	18. y	25. ink	32. ock	
5. am	12. ing	19. out	26. ow	33. ake	
6. ag	13. ap.	20. ug	27. ew	34. ine	
7. ack	14. unk	21. op	28. ore	35. ight	

- **Word Building.** *Word building* (sometimes called onset rime) is a teaching strategy that asks students to build words using onsets and rimes. An *onset* is the first letter or letter blend in the word. In the word *slip* the onset is "sl." In the word *tape* the onset is "t." A *rime* is another name for a word family or phonogram. For example, the rime in the word *tape* is "ape." The rime in the word *slip* is "ip."

Word-building activities can be designed using paper, Power-Points, scrabble letters, or words and letters printed on cards. There are two general types of word-building activities. The first is *onset variations*. Here you work through all the variations of a single phonogram using different onsets (Figure 11.10). To do this, present the onset and rime separately. When the student has combined the parts to create the word, then show the complete word. Then move to the next onset and repeat.

The second is *rime variations*. Here you use a common onset and ask students to make new words by adding different phonograms (see Figure 11.11). This can be done in riddle form. Example: "I've got the /h/ sound.

Figure 11.10   Variations on a Single Phonogram

h—**ay** hay	pay	hay
	day	jay
	lay	ray
ay say	say	stay ay
	may	fray
j—**ay** jay	bay	ray
	gray	play

What phonogram do I need to connect to get some cow food?" or "What word would I get if I added /ip/ to /h/?"

Keep word-building activities simple. Remember, the goal is not to do word-building activities; rather, the goal is to enhance students' ability to automatically recognize parts within words as they read.

Figure 11.11   Variations Using Multiple Phonograms

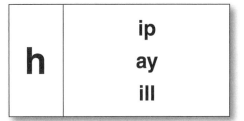

- **Word Walls.** Start by making posters of common phonograms (see Figure 11.12). Here the phonogram should be displayed on top of the column with all variations below. Use your word wall for phonograms to extend this activity by making phonogram riddles. Example: "I'm thinking of a word in the 'in' family. It is something found on a fish." This is a fun and simple way to develop and reinforce students' ability to recognize parts within a word. Eventually, students will be able to create their own riddles. Word walls can also be used for writing or speaking activities. Example: "See if you can create a silly sentence using a word in the /ate/ family." Or, "Think about a sentence using a word in the /in/ family. Turn to your neighbor and tell them your sentence." To extend this, "See if you neighbor can add something interesting to your sentence from the /ate/ family."

Figure 11.12   Word Wall for Phonograms

ay	in	ate
hay	tin	hate
may	bin	late
day	kin	Kate
say	fin	date
lay	pin	fate
pay	win	mate
play	shin	gate

- **Phonogram Treasure Hunts.** Treasure hunts can be used with phonograms as well as vowel sounds, letter blends, grammatical elements, and sight words. Using a book they have already read, students look for specific phonograms. Using a data retrieval chart (Figure 11.13), students put a tally mark in the appropriate column every time

Figure 11.13   Example of DRC for Phonograms

Phonograms		
ay	ip	ill

they encounter an example of the target phonogram. You can extend the activity by having them create bar graphs representing their findings.

• **Dictated Sentences.** To help students recognize familiar phonograms, use dictated writing (see Chapter 10) with sentences that include words with a target phonogram. For example, if you are targeting the /ip/ phonogram, the dictated sentence would be, "I like to sip pop."

MORPHEMIC ANALYSIS

A morpheme is the smallest unit of meaning within a word. This usually refers to prefixes, suffixes, and root words.

Morphemic Analysis: A Strategy for Identifying Words

Morphemic analysis is a strategy whereby students use prefixes, suffixes, and root words to identify unknown words as they read. Very much like word parts above, teach it explicitly using the following steps:

1. Provide a sentence with a target word in it.
2. Ask students if there are prefixes, suffixes, or roots that they recognize.
3. Ask students to use the prefix, suffix, or root to construct a word or to make a guess.
4. Students should reread the sentence using the new word to see if it makes sense.

The Most Common Prefixes and Suffixes

Before students are able to use morphemic analysis, they need to know a bit about prefixes, suffixes, and root words. The 20 most common prefixes in Figure 11.14 account for almost 97% of all prefixed words that students will encounter (White, Sowell, & Yanagihara, 1989). The four most common prefixes account for about 65% of all prefixed words used in school. Thus, it makes sense to focus instruction on these 20 prefixes, with special attention to the first four.

Figure 11.14   Most Common Prefixes

Prefix	Meaning	Example
1. un	not, opposite of	unhappy
2. re	again, back	rebuild, restart, rejoin
3. in, im, ir, il	not, opposite of	insecure, immovable, irrational, illegal
4. dis	not, opposite of, remove	disbelieve
5. en, em	cause to	empower
6. non	not, opposite of	nonsense
7. in, im, in or into	in or into	inbound, immerge
8. over (too much)	too much, above	overstate
9. mis	wrongly	misjudge
10. sub	under, lower	subpar
11. pre	before	pregame
12. inter	between, among	interpersonal
13. fore	before	forerunner
14. de	opposite of, down, remove, reduce	declassify, degrade, deicer, declassify
15. trans	across, change, through	transatlantic, transact, transition, transparent
16. super	above, beyond	superman, superimpose
17. semi	half, partial	semicircle, semiconscious, semiannual, semifinal
18. anti	against	antipoverty
19. mid	middle	midlevel, midstream
20. under	too little, below	underpaid

Likewise, the 20 most common suffixes in Figure 11.15 account for 93% of the suffixed words that students will encounter (White, Sowell, & Yanagihara, 1989). The three most common suffixes make up approximately 64% of all the suffixed words used in school. Thus, it makes sense to focus instruction on these 20 prefixes, with special attention to the first three.

Keep instruction simple. Teach what each of the prefixes and suffixes mean and how they change the meaning of the words to which

Figure 11.15   Most Common Suffixes

Suffix	Meaning	Examples
1. s, es	plural, more than one	dogs
2. ed	past tense	jumped
3. ing	action, process	jumping, singing
4. ly	characteristic of	friendly, jumpy
5. er, or (agent)	person connect with,	teacher, reporter
6. ion, tion, ation, ition	act, process, action	connection, election, inflation
7. able, ible	can be done	enjoyable, edible
8. al, ial	having characteristics of	historical, jovial
9. y	characterized by	jumpy
10. ness	state of, condition of	happiness
11. ity, ty	state	gravity, levity, activity
12. ment	action or process	excitement,
13. ic	having characteristic of	historic,
14. ous, eous, ious	possessing qualities of	curious, hideous, serious
15. en	made of	wooden, frighten, flatten
16. er (comparative)	comparative	smarter, bigger
17. ive, ative, tive	adjective form of a noun	active, attentive, enliven
18. ful	full of	joyful, hurtful
19. less	without	worthless
20. est	comparative	happiest

they are attached. Keep in mind that prefixes and suffixes are not always reliable in terms of their meaning and spelling. For example, *restart* has a "re" prefix but *reveal* does not. *Impatient* has an "im" prefix, but *important* does not. The unreliability of prefixes and suffixes tells us that it's not pragmatic to spend too much time memorizing and drilling definitions. Instead, focus on helping students to recognize or perceive common prefixes and suffixes, knowing that the context in which the word is found along with syntax will provide additional word identification clues.

Teaching About Prefixes

To create a general awareness of common prefixes and suffixes, create simplified versions of Figures 11.14 and 11.15 for posters. When introducing a new prefix, show students the word in the context of a sentence, the new prefix by itself, and the target word without the prefix (see Figure 11.16). Then, define the prefix, show or say the word in the context of a sentence, and help students identify at least two synonymous words or phrases.

Figure 11.16   Examples of How to Introduce New Prefixes to Students

- I was **happy**. I lost my shoes and I was not happy or **unhappy**.

    happy————unhappy

    un + happy = unhappy

- When you are not sick you are **healthy**. When you get sick you are **unhealthy**.

    healthy————unhealthy

    un + healthy = unhealthy

Teaching About Suffixes

Suffixes should be taught in the same way as prefixes. Make sure students see the word with and without the suffix (see Figure 11.17 on the next page). In your initial teaching of suffixes (and prefixes), try not to include any of the spelling anomalies. Look for words (when possible) that change meaning by simply adding the prefix or suffix. For example, in looking at the "est" suffix, I would not make mention of instances of changing the "y" to an "i" as in "happiest" initially. Save that for a later lesson.

Root Words

A root word is the part of the word from which other parts grow, usually by adding a prefix or suffix and sometimes by adding other root words. Sometimes the roots make sense by themselves and sometimes not. Root words usually have their origin in Greek or Latin languages. Most dictionaries provide this type of information

Figure 11.17   Examples of How to Introduce New Suffixes to Students

- I have one **bell**. Molly has two **bells.**

    bell—bells

    bell + s = bells

- Today I will **jump**. Yesterday I **jumped.**

    jump—jumped

    jump + ed = jumped

- I like to **sing**. Right now I am **singing.**

    sing—singing

    sing + ing = singing

regarding root words. As well, there are many online sources for getting information related to root words. (Do an Internet search using the term *etymology*.)

In teaching root words, first provide a very simple definition followed by common examples. Then work with students to identify how each word is related to the root. For example: "Port means to carry, like in the word *portable*. Airport—It carries people and things to different places through the air." You can find many examples of words by doing an Internet search using the following terms: *words-with-*[insert target root]-*in-them*. Finally, create posters for reference and instruction (see Figure 11.18). Refer to these posters often.

So, which root words should you teach? Teach the root words that students encounter in texts, curriculum, discussions, or in the news as the basis for instruction. Again, keep it simple. Remember that students rarely encounter words in isolation. They will always have semantic and syntactical clues as well as morphemic clues to use in identifying words.

Figure 11.18   Poster for Root Words

form—to shape	port—to carry
formula	airport
inform	export
conform	portable
perform	transport
uniform	deport
transform	passport
inform	portfolio

Activities for Developing Morphemic Recognition

Below are some simple activities that can be used to help develop and strengthen students' neural pathways to enhance their ability to recognize morphemes automatically as they read. Also, many of the games and activities described in Chapter 10 can be used here as well.

• **Peel Off.** After a short minilesson on one to three target prefixes, suffixes, or root words, provide examples of the targets in the context of sentences. Ask students to peel off one part and say the word. For example: "Please *review* your homework. Take of the /re/ and what do you get?"

• **Flashcards.** You can play a variety of flashcard games with prefix and suffix words; however, make sure the root word is already in students' reading vocabulary. This is not the place to be introducing new words. The goal of flashcards is to develop the ability to recognize prefix and suffix words instantly. This means that you should flash the cards quickly.

• **Wordo.** This was described in Chapter 10. Use words that include target prefixes and suffixes.

• **Writing Prompts.** Create open-ended, student-centered word prompts using a word that contains the target prefix, suffix, or root word. Example: "I like playing . . . I am happiest when . . . If I could undo the past . . . "

• **Treasure Hunts.** The treasure hunts described above can also be used with prefixes, suffixes, and root words.

• **Multiple Forms.** Present a root word, then show the root in multiple forms. Here is an example: jump, jumping, and jumped. Create posters or have students create posters of common multiple form words. Include a picture (or have students create pictures). This is one of the areas where art and literacy interact (language arts). These would make very interesting mobiles or other art projects.

• **Making Words.** Present a root word. Then present a prefix bank and suffix bank. Let students see how many words they can make using the root word and various prefixes, suffixes, or even other root words. Encourage students to use the Internet for this using the search terms: *words-with*-[target] or *words-containing*-[target].

• **Maze Sentences.** These were described earlier and can be used to focus on prefixes or suffixes. Students must select the correct form of the word. Use this to reinforce the prefix, suffix, or root work with which you are working (see Figure 11.19).

Figure 11.19   Example of a Maze Sentence

He went [**runs, running, ran**] on the path.

• **Word-Split Chart.** Find an interesting word that students will encounter in texts or discussions with a prefix or suffix. Create a word-split chart on a bulletin board or computer, or have students create one in their learning logs (Figure 11.20). One column is used for the root and another column for the prefix or suffix. When students encounter a word in text with a similar element, it is recorded. It does not matter if the prefix, suffix, or root has the exact meaning. With this activity, you are helping students to notice similar letter patterns and word parts.

Figure 11.20   Example of a Word Split Chart

restart	
<u>re</u>	**start**
1. rewind	1. startled
2. review	2. startup
3. reverse	3. kick start
4. reoccur	4. upstart

• **Words With.** Find a common root, such as *rupt* (e*rupt*, *rupt*ure, bank*rupt*cy). Do a web search using the term *words-with*-[insert root] or *words-containing*-[insert root]. Have students select words that are familiar to them to create word banks, word walls, posters, or mind maps.

SIGHT WORDS

Sight words are words that students recognize instantly (on sight) without having to use letter cues, word parts, or context clues. Fluent readers have a large sight-word vocabulary while less-fluent readers have a small sight-word vocabulary. Thus, part of helping less-fluent readers become more fluent involves increasing their sight-word vocabulary.

Just like prefixes and suffixes above, teach the sight words that students will encounter most often. There are a number of lists of most common words, including Dolch, Fry, and Zeno words lists. They are all relatively similar. It doesn't really matter which one you use (see Figure 11.21).

Figure 11.21   Fry 100 Most Frequent Words

___the	___at	___there	___some	___my
___of	___be	___use	___her	___than
___and	___this	___an	___would	___first
___a	___have	___each	___make	___water
___to	___from	___which	___like	___been
___in	___or	___she	___him	___call
___is	___one	___do	___into	___who
___you	___had	___how	___time	___oil
___that	___by	___their	___has	___now
___it	___word	___if	___look	___find
___he	___but	___will	___two	___long
___was	___not	___up	___more	___down
___for	___what	___other	___write	___day
___on	___all	___about	___go	___did
___are	___were	___out	___see	___get
___as	___we	___many	___number	___come
___with	___when	___then	___no	___made
___his	___your	___them	___way	___may
___they	___can	___these	___could	___part
___I	___said	___so	___people	___over

Your approach to the 100 most frequent words (MFW) should be systematic. As described in Chapter 10, this means having a general plan for introducing the words as well as documenting when you have taught them and when students have mastered each word. Instruction should be brief, briskly paced, and as enjoyable as possible. Use games, art projects, and other activities to reinforce these words. You can find a wealth of interesting and effective sight-word activities on the Internet using the terms: *sight-word-activities.*

Last Word

This chapter examined word identification. The following strategies were described:

- Cloze
- Maze
- Writing
- Syntax sentences
- Sentence combing
- Sentence alteration
- Sentence elaboration
- Analyzing practice
- The big word bank
- Comparing words
- Word-building
- Word walls
- Phonogram treasure hunts
- Dictated sentences
- Peel off
- Flashcards
- Wordo
- Writing prompts
- Treasure hunts
- Multiple forms
- Making words
- Maze sentences
- Word split chart
- Words with

There is no single strategy or approach that works best with all students. Select and use the strategies that work best for the students with whom you are working. In helping students to develop the ability to identify words, include strategies that develop all three cueing systems (phonological, syntactic, and semantic). Keep in mind that for every 10 minutes of instruction or teacher-directed activities, there should be 40 to 50 minutes of independent reading practice.

12

Fluency

Repeated practice playing the piano or singing musical text enables musicians to become fluent reading an individual piece of music and also improves their ability to sight read other music. They begin to see musical passages and hear chord progressions instead of individual notes. So it is with alphabetic text.

As stated in earlier chapters, readers struggle because of deficits in one or more of the following three areas: word identification, comprehension, and fluency. This chapter describes strategies that can be used to enhance reading fluency.

READING FLUENCY

Reading fluency is the ability to recognize words automatically during reading. This automatic response, called automaticity, improves comprehension by allowing the reader to spend more thinking space focusing on the meaning of the text and less thinking space trying to process letters and identify individual words (Kuhn & Stahl, 2013).

Reading fluency is also related to speed or rate. Why is rate important? Think about this: A homework assignment that would take average readers about 20 minutes to read and comprehend might take a struggling reader 40 to 60 minutes or more with far less comprehension. That means that struggling readers have to spend twice as long completing daily homework and other assignments. This makes it far less likely that daily assignments will be completed or completed very well.

NEURAL PATHWAYS AND NETWORKS

In Chapter 2, I described neurons, neural pathways, and neural networks. Neurons are brain cells that send and receive information. These become the basis of our thinking. New paths are created between neurons when we first link one thing to another such as letters to sounds, word parts to words, and words to meaning. And just like a path in the snow, the more a path is traveled, the deeper and wider it becomes. Repetition and practice enable us to travel these pathways many times and strengthen the connections. The main purpose of fluency work is to strengthen neural pathways in order to enhance the speed in which we are able to recognize words and process text.

Neurons that are related conceptually or associated in some way are connected in a web or a neural network. As we learn new words and concepts and as we have new experiences, these neural networks expand, connecting to more neurons and other networks. During the process of reading, these neural networks are used to formulate, plan, and direct lower structures to seek out specific information and to confirm or disconfirm predictions (Gilbert & Sigman, 2007; Strauss, 2011; Weaver, 2009). In other words, the higher cortical structures of the brain feed forward information that is used to direct perception, make predictions, and fill in the blanks as we create

Source: Thinkstock/Comstock.

meaning with print (Hruby, 2009;

Strauss, Goodman, & Paulson, 2009). Hence, helping to expand students' neural networks makes them less reliant on letter cues thereby lessening the word processing demands and enhancing fluency. Wide reading is an effective way to do this (see below). A well-designed curriculum that brings students in contact with new words and concepts is also important in providing a solid basis for reading.

STRATEGIES FOR ENHANCING READING FLUENCY

Below are some general tips for enhancing students' reading fluency.

Wide Reading

Reading a lot is one of the best cures for most reading problems including fluency (Allington, 2012; Krashen, 2004). As stated above, it's a highly effective way to expand conceptual and vocabulary knowledge as well as enhance comprehension, word identification, and fluency. However, many struggling readers hate reading. You can hardly blame them when reading is associated with continual failure and frustration. Also, struggling readers are often asked to read books that are written at a reading level too high or an emotional level far below them. High/low books are one solution to this problem (see below). This is the term used for books that are high interest but written at a low-grade level. For example, a book that might appeal to students in grades 5–12 would be written at the third- or fourth-grade level.

  • **High/Very-Low Books.** Severely struggling readers need access to high/very-low books. These are books that are of interest to students in grades 5–12 but written at the first- or second-grade level. They are concept driven and picture based (see Figure 12.1). That is, they are about concepts or topics of interest to students and use pictures to present relevant information. One or two sentences are written beneath each picture to describe it. In this way, students are able to use existing neural networks along with picture information to help create meaning with the text as they read. This is one way of providing scaffolding to make reading accessible to severely struggling readers.

Figure 12.1   Example of a High/Very-Low Book

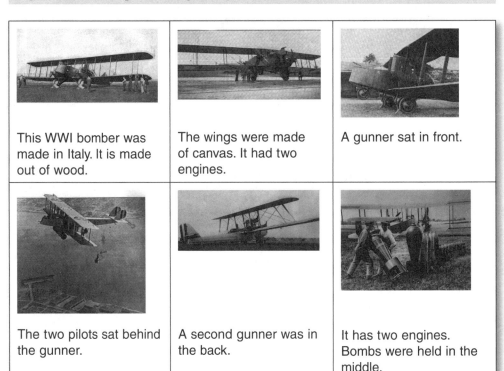

This WWI bomber was made in Italy. It is made out of wood.	The wings were made of canvas. It had two engines.	A gunner sat in front.
The two pilots sat behind the gunner.	A second gunner was in the back.	It has two engines. Bombs were held in the middle.

Source: Images courtesy of www.clipart.com.

- **Create Your Own Books.** Currently, there are few high/very-low books available. However, you can work with students to create your own books. Images found on the Internet can be used here. You can also encourage students to bring in or take their own digital pictures (see Figure 12.2). This enables students to write and create meaningful texts related to their lives and experiences. It also enables you to build a classroom library with interesting books for students to use to practice reading. Digital pictures can be cut and pasted onto a word document and printed out or displayed on a PowerPoint®, Prezi, or other online display formats for students to read using a computer.

- **Graphic Novels, Comic Books, and Comic Strips.** Graphic novels, comic books, and comic strips enable students to use pictures to get a sense of the story. For comic strips, start collecting a series from daily newspapers. Cut and paste to create your own comic strip books. As students begin to identify favorite strips, they can create their own comic strip books.

Figure 12.2   High/Very-Low Book Creation Using Digital Pictures

This is Dave.	Dave likes to have adventures.	He flew in an airplane to Alaska.

He rode a horse up in the mountains.	Then he rode in a boat.	And then he hiked. He had to carry everything with him.

He set up his tent and cooked dinner.	He saw some bear tracks.	He decided to stay in his tent and drink coffee.

• **Teacher Read Alouds.** Daily reading to your students is an important part of a total-literacy program. This exposes them to new vocabulary and concepts as well as sentence structure and story grammar. It also provides rich opportunities for incidental teaching of concepts and vocabulary. Picture books should be your primary reading source in first and second grade. In third grade and above, use chapter books.

Repeated Reading

Repeated reading comes in a variety of forms. Here students improve their ability to recognize words and process letter patterns through reoccurring practice of the same text. It's very much like practicing to play the piano or to read musical text. Through repeated practice, you become fluent at reading an individual piece, but also your ability to sight read other music improves. Repeated reading activities can be done individually, with partners, in small groups, or in a whole-class-group setting. Below are some examples of repeated reading activities.

• **Individual WPM.** WPM stands for words per minute. Use a piece of text or a graded reader at the student's independent reading level. First, read the text through while the student follows along. Ask the student to stop you to identify words that could be problematic as you read. Take a minute to look at and review these problem words. Then, on a starting command, the student reads for one minute. Use a stop watch to time this. The goal is to read and pronounce as many words as possible in one minute. You are not concerned about comprehension here, just speed. (There are other places to focus on comprehension.) Follow along to make sure the student pronounces every word. Give minimal hints or clues only when necessary. Call "stop" at the end of the allotted time. Count and record the number of words the students read after each attempt. (Hint: On your text, mark off every 10 words for easy counting.) Repeat the process twice more. Record the number of words after each attempt. Finally, have the student record the three WPM (words-per-minute) scores on a line graph (see Figure 12.3).

The goal of repeated reading is to strengthen neural pathways in order to develop reading fluency. It also is a positive way for students to demonstrate progress in reading. Here students are able to see their progress as their scores go up from their first to their third attempt and over time. This serves to improve their sense of self-efficacy (believing they can accomplish things with effort), which in turn has a positive effect on academic achievement (Schunk & Zimmeran, 2006).

Repeated reading activities take between five and eight minutes. If fluency is a deficit area, students should do a fluency activity every day. For WPM, I recommend using the same graded reader at least three times. Once students are able to consistently read above the approximate grade-level norms for the graded reader you are using (see Figure 12.4), move up to the next grade level.

Figure 12.3   Repeated Reading Graph Showing Words per Minute

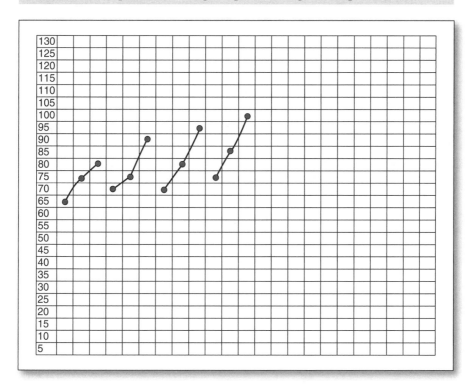

• **Pairs, Small Group, and Whole Class WPM.** In working with pairs and groups, assign each student a partner and a text. Students' texts should be different from their partner and at their independent reading level. On a common signal, one partner reads while the other follows along to make sure every word is read and to help identify problem words. Stop the readers after the allotted time. The nonreading partner should count and record the number of words read. Also, take a minute for the pairs to review problem words. Repeat this two more times and then switch roles. Students then record their times on a graph (see Figure 12.3).

• **WCPM.** WCPM stands for words correct per minute. Here you would count only the words correctly identified in one minute. For the purposes of documenting progress you may wish

Figure 12.4   Approximate Grade Level Fluency Norms

1st grade: 53 WPM
2nd grade: 89 WPM
3rd grade: 107 WPM
4th grade: 123 WPM
5th grade: 139 WPM
6th grade: 150 WPM
7th grade: 150 WPM
8th grade: 151 WPM

to use WCPM; however, for daily fluency activities I would not recommend this. The purpose of fluency activities is to develop speed. There are other ways and places to practice and document word identification accuracy.

- **30WF and 40WF.** 30WF and 40WF stands for 30 word fluency and 40 word fluency. Sometimes students who are reading at the emergent or first-grade level may be overwhelmed by having to read a text for one minute. One solution is to find a story and break it up into exactly 30- or 40-word segments (see Figure 12.5). The student reads each segment through three times and records the time. Each read should take students less than 30 seconds. Just like WPM, document the time after each attempt and have students record their times on a graph (see Figure 12.6). When students are consistently able to read 30WF in 12 seconds or less, move them up to the 40WF. When they are able to consistently read 40WF in 12 seconds or less, they are ready for WPM using text at their independent reading level.

Figure 12.5   30WF and 40WF

30WF	40WF
It was March. There was snow on the ground. Bob said, "I'm sick of the snow." "Me too!" said Sally. "I want it to be summer." "Me too," said Bob.	Sam and Pat were bored. "What do you want to do?" asked Pat. "I don't know," said Sam. "What do you want to do?" "I don't know," said Pat. "What do you want to do?" "I asked first," said Sam.

- **Reread to Meet Goal.** This strategy invites students to work to meet a goal (thereby helping to develop both fluency and a sense of self-efficacy). Start by finding students' approximate WPM score when reading at their independent reading level. Then, set a goal for the student that is just slightly above this. For example, if their average WPM is 55 on a Grade 2 reader, set a goal for the student to read 58 WPM. Then, see how many attempts it takes the student to read the text in order to reach the WPM goal. Record the number of attempts in table form (Figure 12.7).

Figure 12.6   30WF and 40WF Graph

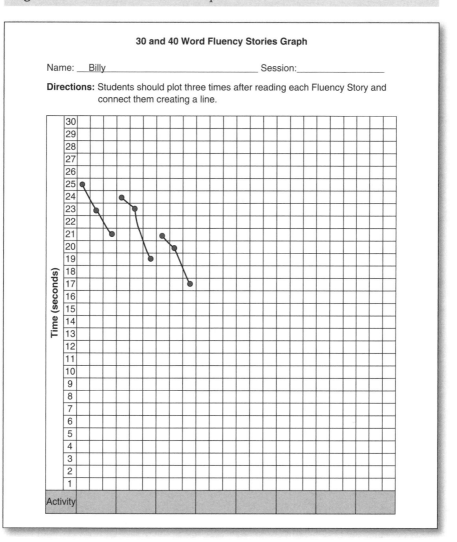

Figure 12.7   Table for Reread to Meet a Goal

Date	Goal	Number of Tries
3/12/14	65 WPM	5
3/14/14	65 WPM	3
3/18/14	65 WPM	2
3/21/14	68 WPM	6
3/26/14	68 WPM	3
3/29/14	68 WPM	2

• **Replay Analysis**. First, get a 25- to 40-word sample of text that is at the student's instructional reading level. Photocopy it so that the student can make marks on it. Next, the student reads the selection out loud into an audio recorder. After reading, the student replays and analyzes his or her oral reading along with the teacher to look for miscues, errors, or mispronunciations. Listening to the recording helps the student determine what makes sense in the context of each sentence. Since the student does not have to focus on decoding words, he or she is better able to concentrate on meaning as well as detect errors or mispronunciations. Then, the student should circle the problem words. Repeat the oral reading, taping, and analysis until the student achieves fluency.

Other Fluency Strategies

• **Echo Reading.** Echo reading is where the teacher reads a line of text and students repeat or echo it back. This is usually done with younger students. It can be done with a big book or regular-sized books, individually or in groups. When using big books, the teacher should point to the words as they are read. With regular size books, have students point to the words as they are read. To enhance fluency, echo read the same piece two or three times, moving a little faster each time.

• **Reader's Theater.** In reader's theater, a familiar story (one they have read), is broken into parts to create a script (see Figure 12.8). You will have to create the initial scripts here, but eventually students will be able to create their own. Students are assigned to different parts. Use

Figure 12.8 Reader's Theater Script

Narrator:	One day Little Red Riding Hood told her mother,
Little Red:	I think I'll walk through the woods to visit Grandma. I haven't seen her for a long time.
Narrator:	Her mother said to her,
Mother:	Be careful Little Red. There may be a wolf in the woods.
Little Red:	Oh Mother. I'm not afraid of any silly, old wolf.
Narrator:	So Little Red started off down the trail through the woods.

narrator and character parts. You can also use students for sound effects. These can be audio taped for use with picture books. (While the words won't match exactly here, the pictures will.) Reader's theater provides opportunities for students to practice reading their lines many times.

• **Conversations.** Dialogue is familiar to students and is usually easier to read than other types of text. To capitalize on this, create your own short conversational dialogs with students (see Figure 12.9). On a PPT or word processer, create two characters. You can use characters from a book, imaginary characters, historical characters, or real life characters. Differentiate the dialogue using different colors for each. Write these by having the conversation with the student and writing down what they say. The student should be able to see the screen as you are recording what they say. Read these through several times until the student can do it fluently. Save them for future reading practice.

Figure 12.9   Conversations

Bob: Hi Gary.	**Pat:** Hi, Chip.
Gary: Hi. Who are you?	**Chip:** Hi, Pat.
Bob: I'm Bob. I'm a magic helper elf.	**Pat:** Do you want to play with me?
	Chip: Yes. What do you want to play?
Gary: You're real?	**Pat:** Let's play cards.
Bob: Of course I'm real. You can see me, can't you?	**Chip:** Okay. What kind of card game should we play?

• **Language Experience Activities (LEA).** This technique was described earlier in Chapter 9. Reread these until the student can read fluently. Save these for future reading practice.

• **Scaffolded Oral Reading (ScORe).** This technique was also described in Chapter 8. Here you read quietly with the student, pushing the pace slightly, and dropping out occasionally. The goal is to provide a slight scaffold.

• **Read Alongs or Follow Alongs.** Use online digital books or recorded versions of other books for students to listen to and either read along or follow along silently as the text is read. I have found, by watching students eyes that they naturally follow along with the text the majority of times.

• **Poems and Song Lyrics.** Poems and popular song lyrics are excellent sources to use for reading practice. For younger students, the predictable or rhyming text found in poems provides the repetition necessary to reinforce letter patterns and help them be successful readers. With older students, the familiarity of popular song lyrics provides the scaffolding necessary to enable them to be successful. These can easily be downloaded and used for reading fluency practice.

The following are directions for using poems and song lyrics for reading practice: First read the poem or lyric with students using ScORe. Then have students read through the lyrics independently until they can read them fluently. Finally, create a mini phonics lesson by asking students to look for words with particular letters, letter patterns, or phonograms. Save these for future reading practice.

AVOID ROUND-ROBIN READING

Round-robin reading is where you go around the classroom or small group and everybody takes a turn reading out loud. Another version of this is called popcorn reading. Here the teacher calls on a student to start reading. When that student finishes the teacher or the student calls on another student to continue reading. In multilevel classrooms round-robin reading is sometimes used so that students who are struggling readers don't fall behind conceptually. In small group reading classes, it is sometimes used to give everybody reading practice. However, there are very few instances where this is an effective or appropriate strategy. Students are more concerned about not making a mistake than creating meaning; thus, you end up with a lot of word-by-word reading. This inhibits more than promotes reading fluency and comprehension. As well, it doesn't reflect real reading. (I have never seen people sitting around the table taking turns reading orally in a library or other places in the real world.) It also creates heightened anxiety for students who are struggling readers. While there are times and places to have students read out loud, there are very few instances where round-robin reading is appropriate. Avoid this whenever possible.

Last Word

This chapter examined strategies related to fluency. The following strategies were described:

- High/very-low books
- Graphic novels, comic books, and comic strips
- Teacher read alouds
- Individual WPM
- Pairs, small group, and whole class WPM
- WCPM
- 30WF and 40WF
- Reread to meet goal
- Replay analysis
- Echo reading
- Reader's theater
- Language experience activities (LEA)
- Scaffolded oral reading (ScORe)
- Read alongs or follow alongs
- Poems and song lyrics

The main purpose of fluency work is to strengthen neural pathways in order to enhance the speed in which students are able to recognize words. Again, this requires practice and repetition. However, practice and repetition should take place in meaningful contexts (authentic reading) whenever possible. That is, students should be reading authentic texts using words and concepts that are largely familiar to them when working on fluency. This is done for two reasons: First, this strengthens neural pathways within existing neural networks. And second, practicing in authentic contexts makes it much more likely students will be able to transfer these skills to similar contexts.

13

Comprehension of Narrative Text

> *Nobody in real life cares if students can identify story grammar elements. It's not at all important. What is important is that the related cognitive process becomes automatic during the act of reading narrative text.*

This chapter focuses on strategies to enhance the comprehension of narrative text. The next chapter focuses on comprehending expository text.

COMPREHENSION BASICS

Comprehending is the act of understanding what you read. In other words, comprehension involves creating meaning. Here are six basic ideas:

1. **Comprehension is an active process** (Almasi, Palmer, Madden, & Hart, 2011; Sousa, 2014). Good readers have to do something to

construct meaning as they read. At varying degrees they use background knowledge along with a variety of thinking processes.

2. **Background knowledge is an integral part of comprehending** (Jensen, 2005; Neuman, 2006). Meaning is constructed as we bring what we know to what we read. Again, we use what's in our head to understand what's on the page.

3. **Comprehension involves thinking** (Jennings, Caldwell, & Lerner, 2010). Figure 13.1 lists some of the cognitive operations used by effective readers (Lipson & Wixon; 2009, Tompkins, 2011). These cognitive operations are the basis for the activities in the next two chapters.

Figure 13.1 Cognitive Operations Used by Effective Readers

1. Compare	7. Problem solve	14. Recognize story grammar
2. Respond aesthetically	8. Analyze	
3. Infer	9. Evaluate	15. Reflect: metacognition
4. Identify important ideas or themes	10. Make connections	16. Visualize
5. Identify supporting details	11. Order	17. Question
6. Identify cause-effect relationships	12. Inductive analysis	18. Summarize
	13. Predict	

4. **We can improve comprehension by improving thinking** (Almasi et al., 2011; Dole, Nokes, & Drits, 2009; Martin & Kuke, 2011). Attending to students' cognitive operations before, during, and after reading enhances their ability to comprehend what they read. This doesn't happen in one or two lessons; rather, it happens over time.

5. **Efficient readers approach narrative and expository text differently** (Allington & McGill-Franzen, 2009; Rosenblatt, 1983). Narrative texts are descriptions of events. These include fiction, such as fairytales, plays, fantasy, detective stories, thrillers, science fiction, and romance. It also includes nonfiction, such as biographies, autobiographies, memoirs, diaries, and personal recollections. Expository texts describe information and ideas. This could include things such as informational books, articles, editorials, encyclopedias, websites, dictionaries, manuals, directions, magazines, or newspapers.

6. **Teachers should design different types of activities for narrative and expository text differently** (Cunningham & Allington, 2010; Rosenblatt, 1983). The usual purpose for reading narrative text is to be entertained. Questions and activities should generally reflect an aesthetic response (see Figure 13.2). The purpose for reading expository text is to be informed, to understand, or to build new knowledge. Questions and activities here should generally reflect an efferent response in which students' attention is directed toward information to be learned and remembered.

Figure 13.2   Aesthetic Response Questions and Activities

Aesthetic response questions and activities are designed to invite students to enter into the story, to relive it in some way, to experience the story on an emotional level, or to create associations and connections to real-life events or experiences. The prompts below reflect this type of aesthetic response. These can be used for class discussion, small group activities, journal entries, or as writing prompts.

1. Describe a part of the story that you find interesting or important.
2. Describe a time when you had a similar situation or feeling as one described in the story.
3. Which character is your favorite or least favorite? Why?
4. What questions would you like to ask the author?
5. Compare yourself to one of the characters. How are you alike? How are you different?
6. What were you thinking about as you read today?
7. Draw an interesting or exciting book cover for this story.
8. Create a poster or advertisement that might convince others to read this story.
9. Describe something that might happen after the story has ended.
10. What are three interesting or important things that happened in this story?
11. Ask a question of one of the characters in this story and write what you think the character's answer might be.
12. Describe a problem a character in your book faces and predict how you think that character will solve it.
13. Write a journal entry for one of the characters found in this book.

14. If you appeared some place in this story, what might you see? What might you do?

15. Write a newspaper headline and an article for an event in this book.

16. Draw a picture, create a diagram, or design a symbol that might represent an interesting or important part of this story.

17. Pretend you are one of the characters in this book. Write a letter from that character to you telling about recent events.

18. Record a short dialogue in which you talk with somebody in this book.

TEACHING TIPS

The comprehension activities described below are most effective when used with reading material in which students are able to identify 98% or more of the words (independent reading level). In this way students are able to focus solely on comprehension and don't have to worry about word identification.

When teaching any cognitive process start by providing explicit instruction in a large group (Johnson, 2000). Use cognitive modeling to think out loud as you demonstrate and model. Do this several times (over several lessons). Eventually, you can have students work in pairs and small groups. This is an important part of learning as it enables them to hear the thoughts of others. After students seem familiar with the process, have them practice independently. Remember that developing these cognitive processes occurs over time.

ACTIVITIES ORGANIZED BY COGNITIVE PROCESS

This section describes activities to be used with narrative text. However, the goal is not for students to be able to master each of the activities; rather, the goal is to automatize the cognitive process related to comprehending narrative text. For example, the first series of activities below are related to recognizing various story grammar elements. However, in reality, nobody really cares if you can identify the characters, settings, and events in a story. So why are we doing it? We teach these strategies so that during the act of reading students automatically look for and recognize these elements. Expert readers do this automatically. Teaching students to attend to these elements enhances their ability to comprehend narrative text (Stetter & Hughes, 2010). Again, you are teaching the process to develop the skill.

Recognize Story Grammar

Story grammar refers to structural elements such as characters, setting, events, conflict or problem, and resolution. As stated above, understanding and recognizing story grammar elements enhances students' ability to comprehend narrative text. Start with just three basic story grammar elements: characters, settings, and events (see Figure 13.3). Add additional elements only after students demonstrate mastery of these.

• **Story Grammar as Pre-Reading.** Introduce the basic story grammar elements utilizing the graphic organizer in Figure 13.3 as a form of story preview. This provides students a sense of the story before reading and enhances comprehension.

Figure 13.3   Story Grammar as a Post-Reading Activity

Story Grammar		
Characters	**Settings**	**Events**
1.	1.	1.
2.	2.	2.
3.	3.	3.

• **Story Grammar During Reading.** Introduce just some of the story grammar elements during your pre-reading activity. Then ask students to identify and record other elements as they are encountered in the story.

• **Problem-Solution, Conflict-Resolution.** When students seem to have mastered characters, settings, and events, introduce problem-solution and conflict-resolution as part of story grammar. Teach them to first identify the problem or conflict. A problem is any situation in which there is a difference between the current situation and the ideal. A conflict is any situation in which two or more characters want different actions to be taken or strive for different outcomes. To extend this, have students find the solutions or resolutions.

Predict

Ken Goodman described reading as a psycholinguistic guessing game (Goodman, 1986). Effective readers naturally predict as they are reading. The activities here are all designed to develop this cognitive process.

• **Predict-O-Graph.** Predicting is different from guessing. Predicting is using clues or background information to calculate or deduce what might happen. The graphic organizer in Figure 13.4 can be used to support students' thinking process here. To use the predict-O-graph, stop at a designated point in the story or at the end of a chapter. Give students a prediction question. Example: "What do you think will happen when . . ." Before predicting, students need to list at least two story clues and any background knowledge they think is important. Finally, they should make their prediction based on the story clues and background knowledge.

Figure 13.4   Predict-O-Graph

Predict-O-Graph
What do you think happen when. . . .
Clues
1.
2.
3.
Your prediction:

- **Semantic Impression**. This is a teacher-directed pre-reading activity. Here you provide the title of the story along with a list of eight to ten key words and phrases that represent characters, key events, or settings from the story. Ask students to review these to provide a general impression or prediction of what the story might be about (this can also be used for expository text). Again, the discussion that occurs provides a chance for students to interact with or clarify words, concepts, and events they will encounter before reading.

Visualize

Reading and comprehending narrative text is highly dependent on your ability to create or imagine mental images as you read. The activities here are designed to develop this cognitive process.

- **Stop and Visualize**. At designated places in the story, ask students to describe the mental image in their head. Sample visualization questions are listed in Figure 13.5. Students can write, draw, or simply share their visualizations orally.

Figure 13.5 Sample Visualization Questions

1. What do you see?
2. What does [*character*] look like?
3. What does [*setting*] look like?
4. Describe what [*character*] is wearing.
5. Describe where you think [*character*] lives.
6. Describe what it looks like when [*event*].

- **Enhancing Mental Images.** To extend and enhance the visualization above, have students trade their written descriptions or pictures with another student in small group. Ask students to add one item or thing to the written description or picture before passing it to the next person.

- **Around the World.** This is a post-reading activity. Identify an event or specific place in the story. In a small group, the first person says, "In this scene I see . . ." and inserts something that could logically be found in that scene. The second person repeats the phrases with the first person's item and adds another. The goal is to keep it going as long as possible. The activity ends when students either cannot remember the previous elements or cannot think of anything else to add to the scene.

Infer

To infer is to make a logical extension or conclusion based on story clues. Good readers go beyond the descriptions found in the story or text to fill in some of the story details as they are reading in order to understand ideas not explicitly stated in the text. The activities here are designed to develop this cognitive process.

• **Pre- and During-Reading Infer-O-Graph.** Like the prediction above, an inference is not simply a guess. It's a conclusion based on known information. The infer-O-graph in Figure 13.6 helps organize students' thinking as they learn this skill. As a pre-reading activity, provide an inference question before reading. Tell students to identify and list clues that might help them make this inference as they are reading. A good inference question is one in which there are enough clues found within the text to answer but does not have a specific answer. After reading the story, students should list their inference.

Figure 13.6   Infer-O-Graph

Infer-O-Graph
Interence question:
Clues
1.
2.
3.
Your inference:

• **Post-Reading Infer-O-Graph**. Post-reading inferences works best if students are able to share ideas in pairs or small groups. Again, the discussion that takes place is an important part of developing this cognitive process. Continue this activity until students have completed their discussion. Finally, ask students to decide upon an inference and post their completed infer-O-graph on the board or wall.

• **Character Traits.** As a pre-reading activity, identify one or two characters from the story and two to four character traits (see Figure 13.7). Next, provide a very brief overview of each character and show students the character-rating chart. Then ask them to think about how they would rate the characters on each trait as they read. After reading, move students into pairs or small groups to rate each character. This activity invites students to go beyond the written text, to infer, and to look for clues to support their rating as they are reading.

Figure 13.7   Character Rating Chart

From the Same Book			
	Brave	**Smart**	**Magical**
Harry Potter			
Ron			
Hermione			

Key: 10 = very high; 5 = average; 1 = very low

Compare

The two comparison activities here are both post-reading activities; however, the charts should be introduced as part of a pre-reading activity.

• **Comparison Chart.** The comparison chart in Figure 13.8 is a graphic organizer for comparing and contrasting any two things: characters, events, books, or stories. It's similar to the Venn diagram but provides more structure. When comparing and contrasting, start with similarities in the center column. Then list differences in the outer columns.

• **Comparing T-Chart.** A comparing T-chart (see Figure 13.9) is a simple a way to compare any two characters, items, story events, chapters, or stories side by side. By including themselves students are able to make very personal connections to the story.

Figure 13.8   Comparison Chart

Comparison Chart

Harry Potter	↓ Similarities ↓	Luke Skywalker
• uses a wand • earth • present • learns at school	• didn't know parents • friends to help • gain special powers • battles evil • has to learn things	• uses a lightsaber • space • future • learns from Jedi master

↑   ↑

Differences   **Differences**

Figure 13.9   Graphic Organizer for Making Comparisons

Comparing T-Chart

My Bad Day	Billy Marble's Bad Day
Got up late	Ripped pants
Corn flakes were soggy	Crashed bike
Got yelled at on the bus	Crabby
Lost my homework	Teacher sent him to the office
Got teased at recess	Lost shoes on the playground
Dropped the ball in gym	Space alien tried to capture him

Ideas: Both Billy and I had bad days. His day was worse than mine.

Evaluate

An evaluation is a formal assessment or critique based on a set of criteria. The key is to first identify a set of criteria.

• **Book Critique.** Here students provide an overall assessment of a story based on a set of criteria. As a pre-reading activity, ask students, "What makes a good book?" Identify and record three or four student ideas (see Figure 13.10). (This will naturally lead to the discovery and discussion of genres as students realize that different kinds of stories have different kinds of elements.) Next, provide a brief story preview and tell students they will be rating the story on their criteria after reading. As a post-reading activity, put students in pairs or small groups to rate the story on each criterion.

Figure 13.10 Graphic Organizer for Evaluating Stories

Critique-O-Rater

A good story has the following:

1. Exciting action

2. A happy ending

3. A hero or heroine

4. Characters that you like

	1. Exciting Action	2. Happy Ending	3. Strong Hero or Heroine	4. Characters We Like	Total
The Adventures of Billy Marble	4	4	5	4	17

Key: 5 = very high; 4 = high; 3 = neutral; 2 = low; 1 = very low

Conclusion: This is a pretty good story. We recommend it.

• **Comparing Books.** To extend the book critique, use the graphic organizer in Figure 13.11 to evaluate and compare more than one story. If you are using a basal, this makes a good end-of-unit activity.

• **Generic Book Rating.** The generic book rating may be more appropriate for younger readers (see Figure 13.12). Here students simply provide a rating for the story with an open-ended prompt. These should be posted on a wall or bulletin board. These always lead to interesting discussions that often entice students to read books they may not ordinarily consider.

Figure 13.11   Graphic Organizer for Evaluating and Comparing Stories

Compare-O-Rater

A good story has the following:

1. Exciting action
2. A happy ending
3. A hero or heroine
4. Characters that you like

	1. Exciting Action	2. Happy Ending	3. Strong Hero or Heroine	4. Characters We Like	Total
The Adventures of Billy Marble	4	4	5	4	18
Harry Potter	5	2	4	4	15
Beezus and Ramona	3	5	3	5	16

Key: 5 = very high; 4 = high; 3 = neutral; 2 = low; 1 = very low

Conclusion: We like *The Adventures of Billy Marble* the best.

Figure 13.12   Generic Rating/Review Form for Individual Book Reviews

Name of Book:
Rating: 1 . . . . 2 . . . . . 3 . . . . . 4 . . . . . 5 *Stinker*   *The Best*
What do you tell people about this story?
Reviewer:

Analyze

Analysis is a detailed examination of the elements or structure of something. There are three analytic activities described here.

• **Story Analysis.** Before reading, provide a story preview and tell students to look for interesting or important events. These can be recorded during reading or after. Then, have students decide what events belong in the beginning, middle, and end. Use a simple story analysis chart to organize their thinking here. As Figure 13.13 shows, you can use a variety of types of categories here. Like all comprehensive activities, the end product is not nearly as important as developing the cognitive processes used to identify and analyze story events.

Figure 13.13   Story Analysis Chart

Analyzing Story Parts

List interesting or important events that occurred in each part of the story.

Beginning	Middle	End

List interesting or important events that occurred in the story. Analyze and organize in terms of their importance.

Really Important	Important	Not Important

• **Plot Profile.** The plot profile can be used with individual chapters or with complete books. Students begin by recording interesting or important events that occurred in the story. These are then put in chronological order along the bottom of a line graph (see Figure 13.14). The vertical axis is numbered from one to ten and is used to rate each event on some sort of criteria (happy or sad, exciting or boring, good or bad, or important or not important). Each event is then rated and plotted on the graph. Points on the graph are connected with a line to show change over time.

Figure 13.14   Plot Profile

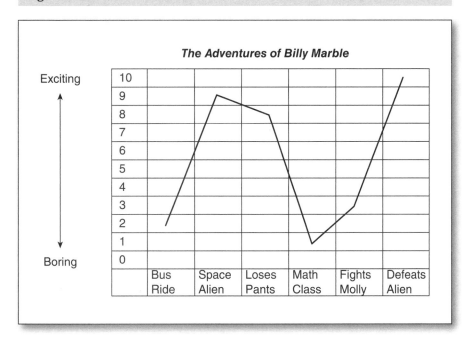

• **Story Map**. A story map is a visual representation of the story plot that lays out the story events so that you can see them in relation to each other (see Chapter 5). Story maps come in a variety of forms. The story map in Figure 13.15 can be used as a pre-reading activity. Create a visual representation of the interesting or important events in the upcoming book or chapter. This provides structure and an overview to enhance students' comprehension as they read the story independently. It can then be used as a during- or post-reading activity. Here students list interesting or important things related to each event. The goal is to enable students to design and create their own post-reading story maps. Story maps are open-ended activities in which students at all levels can experience some level of success.

Identify Cause-Effect

• **Cause-Effect-O-Graph.** As a pre-reading activity, introduce the events of the story found on the cause-effect-O-graph (see Figure 13.16). As students read the story, they identify either the cause or the effect of the events they fill in the graph.

Figure 13.15   Story Map as Pre-Reading Activity

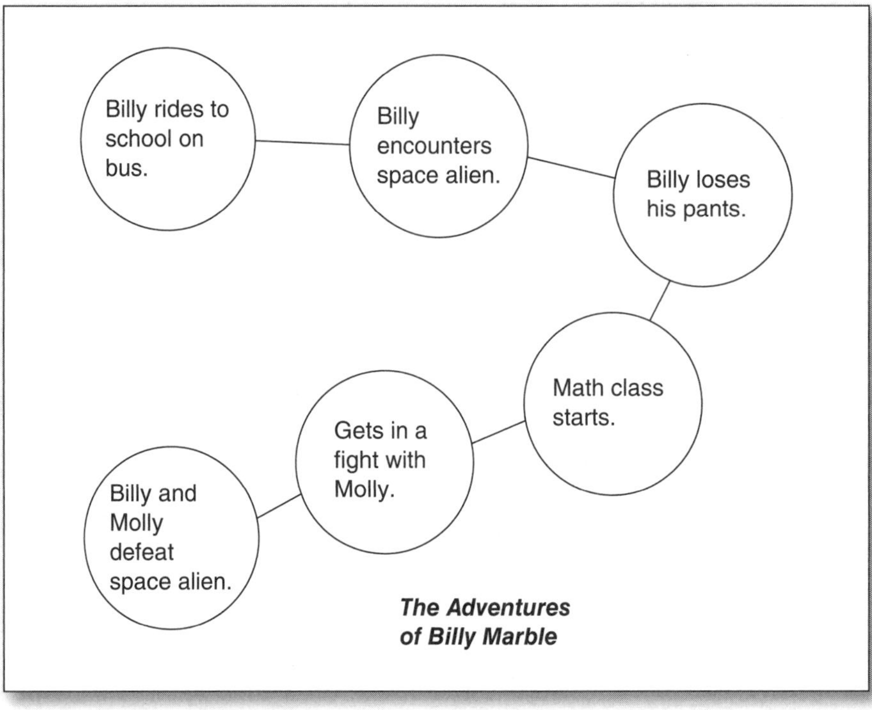

Billy rides to school on bus.

Billy encounters space alien.

Billy loses his pants.

Math class starts.

Gets in a fight with Molly.

Billy and Molly defeat space alien.

The Adventures of Billy Marble

Figure 13.16   Cause-Effect-O-Graph

Cause-Effect-O-Graph	
• Cause = what made it happen (it happened first) • Effect = what happened next	
Cause **(what made it happen)**	**Effect** **(what happened next)**
Bus hits a bump in the road.	
	Billy loses his pants.
Billy falls asleep.	
	Billy and Molly fight.
Billy and Molly defeat the space alien.	

Identify Supporting Details

• **Support-A-Statement.** As a pre-reading activity, introduce a declarative statement related to some aspect of the story along with the support-A-statement graphic organizer (see Figure 13.17). The statement could be factual such as "Billy Marble is brave." It could also be speculative such as "Billy Marble should have stayed home." Tell students to look for supporting ideas as they read the story. As a post-reading activity, students review the text and identify ideas that support the statement. These supporting ideas are then listed under the original statement. Support-A-statement graphic organizers can be made into posters or other types of art works, or written in a journal or literary log. To extend the idea, have students write a paragraph using some or all of the ideas from the support-A-statement.

Figure 13.17   Graphic Organizer for Making and Supporting Statements

---

Support-A-Statement

Statement: Billy Marble should have stayed home.

Supporting Ideas

1. He lost his pants.
2. He was captured by a space alien.
3. He got in a fight with Molly.

• **Character Maps.** Character maps are a pre- or post-reading activity in which students read to find supporting details for character adjectives. As a pre-reading activity, introduce the character and a basic character map with one to three adjectives (see Figure 13.18). As students read the story or after, they look for story details to support the adjectives assigned to the character. Eventually, students will be

Figure 13.18   Character Map

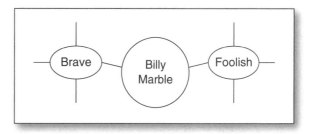

able to identify their own adjectives for story characters. It works best if you assign different story characters to different students, pairs, or small groups. Each would then create a poster of their character for display on the board or wall.

Last Word

This chapter examined strategies to develop cognitive processes related to comprehending narrative text. The following strategies were described:

- Story grammar as pre-reading
- Story grammar during reading
- Problem-solution, conflict-resolution
- Predict-O-graph
- Semantic impression
- Stop and visualize
- Enhancing mental images
- Around the world
- Pre- and during-reading infer-O-graph
- Post-reading infer-O-graph
- Character traits
- Comparison chart
- Comparing T-chart
- Book critique
- Comparing books
- Generic book rating
- Story analysis
- Plot profile
- Story map
- Cause-effect-O-graph
- Support-A-statement
- Character maps

The goal for all the activities described here is to develop cognitive processes so that students engage in these automatically as they read. Again, it is not important that students master any of the activities contained in this chapter. Rather, we teach the process and engage in the activities to enable students to develop the cognitive skill.

14

Comprehension of Expository Text

We cannot expect that students will know how to read expository text unless we teach them how to do so using direct and explicit instruction.

EXPOSITORY TEXT

Starting in about fourth grade, most of the texts that students read are expository texts (McCormick, 2003). These tend to be more difficult to read because of the more formal language, the specialized vocabulary, and the new or unfamiliar concepts involved. But in most classrooms very little time is spent teaching students how to comprehend expository text (Reutzel & Cooter, 1996). This is especially true of special education and remedial settings where the majority of time is spent on decoding accuracy and oral reading fluency (Allington & McGill-Franzen, 2009; Bentum & Aaron, 2003; Swanson & Vaugh, 2010).

This chapter describes three kinds of strategies: (a) pre-reading strategies that teachers can use to prepare students to read expository text, (b) specific study skill strategies for reading expository texts, and

(c) pedagogical strategies to enhance and develop cognitive processes related to the comprehension of expository text.

TEACHER PRE-READING STRATEGIES

Very rarely should you give students a text to read cold (without any sort of preparation). This is especially true for students who are struggling readers. The scaffolded reading experience (SRE) lesson in Chapter 5 described nine activities that teachers can use to get students ready to read a selection independently. Of these, five can be adapted specifically for expository text: (a) activate relevant schemata, (b) preteach or provide background information, (c) identify and teach important vocabulary words, (d) use advanced organizers, and (e) create short discussions related to some aspect of the upcoming selection. Below are some additional strategies that can be used to prepare students to read expository text.

   • **List, Group, and Map**. This works best in small groups or pairs. First, ask students to list what they know about the text topic before reading. Ideas should be listed on the board or written down by one person in a small group setting. Next, ask students to put the ideas into groups. A group consists of two or more things that are related somehow. Each item can only go into one group. Finally, using the text topic as the center, have students create a semantic map using the information on their list (see Figure 14.1). (Make sure they leave enough room to add additional information.) As a post-reading activity, students should add additional information, pictures, or diagrams. It is common for students to do some error correcting at this stage as a result of reading the text. Error correcting is one type of brain-based learning activity recommended by Eric Jensen (2005).

   • **Outlines.** Create and present an outline of the text to students before reading. The goal here is to provide the structure necessary to enable students to independently create meaning with the upcoming selection. The level of detail contained in the outline should be commensurate with students' reading level and age. Severely struggling readers will need more structure; mildly struggling readers will need less. The structure and sequence of information contained in the outline should replicate exactly what is found in the text. The outline can be printed out in paper form, displayed on a board, or projected onto a screen. Also, it may be helpful to preteach some of the more important text elements as you go over the outline before reading.

• **Semantic Maps and Concept Maps.** A *semantic map* displays concepts in a way that shows their relationship to other concepts or ideas (see Figure 14.1). A *concept map* is a top-down representation showing the relationship between concepts. (Chapter 15 will describe how to use these in the context of vocabulary instruction.) Many students prefer maps over the outline because they provide a more visual representation of the information.

Figure 14.1   Semantic and Concept Maps

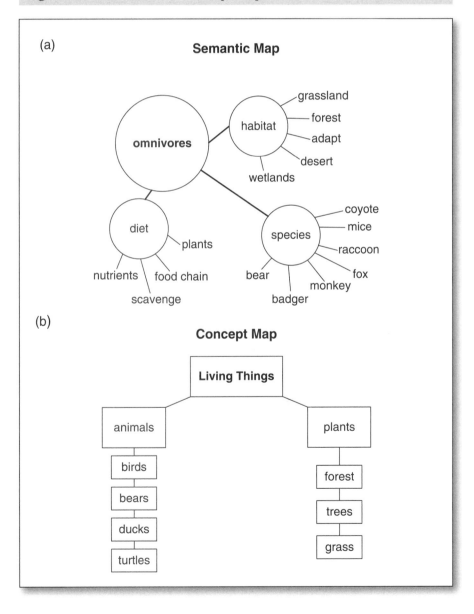

• **Guided Notes.** Guided notes are created by using outlines, semantic maps, or concept maps with spaces provided for students to insert notes as they are reading. Figure 14.2 provides an example of what guided notes could look like for the section below. If I wanted to provide further scaffolding, I would fill in parts of the outline for students.

Figure 14.2   Guided Notes

Study-Skill Strategies

I. Basic Study-Skill Strategies

   A. 5-step basic note-taking strategies

      1.

      2.

   B. Read, dot, and record

      1.

      2.

   C. Preview-overview

      1.

      2.

• **What's My Topic?** This strategy is designed to activate relevant schemata in a game-like format. The topic of the upcoming text should be a mystery. Students are put in small groups and given a clue as to the topic. In turn, each group asks a yes/no question and attempts to guess the mystery topic. Keep going until one group correctly guesses the topic and wins the game.

• **Confirmations.** As a pre-reading activity, present students with three to five declarative statements that can be confirmed by reading the upcoming selection. Students must agree or disagree with each of the statements before reading (see Figure 14.3). They should revise confirmations as needed after reading. This is a good small-group activity.

• **Semantic Impression.** (See Chapter 13.)

Figure 14.3   Confirmations

	Agree	Disagree
1. Crocodiles are amphibians.		
2. Crocodiles cool themselves by opening their mouth.		
3. Crocodiles only live in Australia.		
4. Crocodiles can live to be 80 years old.		
5. An alligator is the same as a crocodile.		

STUDY-SKILL STRATEGIES

A study-skill strategy is a process consciously employed by students to help them create meaning with expository text. Direct and explicit instruction must be used in the teaching of these. For students to adopt and used a strategy, it must be simple, pragmatic, and effective. This section contains seven such study-skill strategies that can be taught to students at all levels.

Basic Study-Skill Strategies

• **5-Step Basic Note-Taking Strategy.** When teaching note-taking strategies, first introduce and use guided notes (above). This provides the structure necessary for students to develop their own note-taking strategy. Then teach a very basic form of note taking. Keep it simple. Students will naturally develop more complex forms of note taking as the need arises.

I recommend teaching the basic 5-step note-taking strategy in Figure 14.4.

• **Read, Dot, and Record.** Sometimes, when reading expository text you want to document the important ideas without interrupting the reading flow by stopping to record notes. For this study skill strategy, put a dot in the margin of the text with a pencil to note important ideas as you are reading. (You can go back and erase the dots later.) This enables you to quickly continue reading without interrupting your flow. After reading, go back and take notes using the 5-step basic note-taking strategy above.

Figure 14.4   The 5-Step Basic Note Taking Strategy

1. Write the title of the article or chapter on top of the page.
2. Write the name of the heading (underline it).
3. As you read each paragraph, select only the most important ideas.
4. Record the idea using short, abbreviated (incomplete) sentences.
5. Record supporting ideas below sentences.
   a. Use numerals for main ideas.
   b. Use small letters for supporting ideas.
   c. This is less confusing than official "outlining" format.

• **Preview-Overview.** Start by reading the first paragraph, the headings and subheading, and the last paragraph. Then read the entire text and take notes. The graphic organizer in Figure 14.5 can be used to teach this process. The first two sections are used to list ideas found in the first and last paragraphs. The last section is used for notes.

Figure 14.5   Graphic Organizer for Preview-Overview

First Paragraph	Last Paragraph
Headings and Notes	

• **Read and Pause.** First, read a paragraph. Then pause to see if you understood and can restate an important idea. If so, resume reading. If not, return and reread.

• **Paragraph Reread.** Read a paragraph. Then skim to find an important idea. Continue.

• **3 × 5 Card.** A 3 × 5 card helps to keep you focused as you read. Some prefer to put the card on top of the line they are reading and move down. This allows their eyes to naturally predict and move ahead. Others prefer to put the card underneath the line they're reading. This can also be used in conjunction with any of the strategies described above.

• **Skim, Reread, and Note.** Quickly skim the text to get a sense of the whole. Then they reread and take notes as you read.

Helping All Teachers Become Teachers of Reading

Below are three simple things that all teachers can do to become "teachers of reading" and effectively help their students comprehend expository text:

1. Use one of the teacher pre-reading strategies described above before assigning any chapter or article for students to read. These pre-reading strategies generally take two to ten minutes.

2. Never assume, at any level, that students know how to read expository text. Starting at the beginning of each year teach one or two of the study skill strategies described in this section. Keep it simple and practical. Don't be afraid to adopt and adapt. Encourage students to use the ones that work best for them.

3. Create a poster that has the study-skill strategies that you will teach in your classes (see Figure 14.6 on the next page). Break each study-skill strategy into specific steps. When assigning a text, always remind students to use one of these study-skill strategies.

PEDAGOGICAL STRATEGIES TO DEVELOP COGNITIVE PROCESSES RELATED TO COMPREHENSION

This section describes pedagogical strategies that are designed to develop cognitive processes related to comprehending expository text (see Figure 14.1 on page 187). Like the last chapter, mastering the activities below is relatively unimportant. What is important is automatizing the related cognitive processes during the act of reading expository text.

• **3-I Chart.** This activity can be done in small group, pairs, or individually. After reading the text, ask students to identify what they consider to be the interesting or important ideas (3-I). It works best if

Figure 14.6 Poster Ideas for Study-Skill Strategies

Take Notes	Dot and Notes	Preview-Overview	Skim, Reread, and Note
1. Record a heading. 2. Read a paragraph. 3. Record important ideas. 4. Use numbers and letters.	1. Read a paragraph. 2. Put dot next to important ideas. 3. Finish chapter 4. Take notes using an outline and headings.	1. Look at the title and headings. 2. Read the first paragraph and last paragraphs. 3. Read the article or chapter. 4. Take notes.	1. Quickly skim read the article or chapter. 2. Reread the article or chapter. 3. Note or record important ideas.
Paragraph Reread 1. Read each paragraph quickly. 2. Reread to find important sentences or ideas. 3. Continue reading.	**3 × 5 Card** 1. Put a card on the top or bottom of the sentence. 2. Move slowly ahead as you read.	**Read and Pause** 1. Read a paragraph. 2. Pause and check. (Do I understand?) 3. Return or resume reading.	

you can identify a specific number. ("Boys and girls, find at least three ideas that you believe are interesting or important."). This empowers students to make the decision as to what might be interesting or important. (There will be other places for students to summarize and support specific ideas and to check for comprehension.) Also, this open-ended format enables students of all ability levels to succeed, and it also provides insight as to how students are processing this text. The 3-I chart can be recorded in a journal or reading log. It can also be display on a wall or bulletin board using a poster or large chart (see Figure 14.7). Encourage students to add pictures or diagrams to their 3-I chart.

• **3-I Look Back.** This strategy works best in individual tutoring sessions with students who tend to read too quickly. It can also be adopted for use in pairs or small groups (see below). After reading

Figure 14.7   3-I Chart

3-I Chart

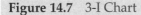

Interesting or important ideas (or events or facts):

---

a page or a paragraph, the student must identify an interesting or important idea before moving on. The text should be available for students to use to skim for look backs.

- **Double Look Back**. Here students are paired with a partner to read the assigned text. They stop after every page or paragraph. One of them must identify an interesting or important idea before moving on. As they continue, the next person identifies an interesting or important idea. The conversation that naturally arises from this is an important part of the learning process here.

- **Reciprocal Reading.** Reciprocal reading is a slight variation on double look back. Students are again paired with a partner to read expository text. After every page or paragraph, the pair stops. One partner covers the page and explains what they've just read to the other partner. The other partner looks at the page and includes any missing parts. They continue to the next page or paragraph and switch roles. This strategy invites students to attend to what they're reading and to monitor comprehension. Figure 14.8 contains the steps for this simplified form of reciprocal reading.

- **3-I Pre-Post**. In a large group, small group, or individually, students generate a list of things they know about the text topic before reading. Let them know that they will be looking for interesting or important ideas to add after reading. After reading, students identify what they believe to be interesting or important ideas. Use the graphic organizers in Figure 14.9. Leave a section in the middle for pictures or diagrams.

Figure 14.8   Simplified Version of Reciprocal Reading

Reciprocal Reading

1. Two partners read material.

2. Stop after reading a designated amount (page, paragraph, or section).

3. Partner #1 covers the page and summarizes or explains.

4 Partner #2 checks for accuracy and includes any missing material.

5. Partners read the next page, paragraph, or section.

6. Reverse roles.

Figure 14.9   3-I Pre-Post

Things I know about crocodiles:

1.

2.

Interesting or important ideas about crocodiles:

1.

2.

• **Preview and Predict**. First, have students review the title, headings, pictures, and diagrams. Then, make predictions as to what sorts of things will be covered in this text. List their predictions on a board or paper. Finally, after reading, put a check mark next to all the accurate predictions.

• **Connections.** Introduce the text topic found in the upcoming selection before reading. Before reading, tell students that they will be asked to make four kinds of connections (see Figure 14.10): (a) connect the topic to something similar, (b) make an association, (c) connect the text topic to a real life encounter, and (d) draw or insert a picture or diagram related to the text topic.

Figure 14.10   Connect-O-Izer

It is like . . .	It reminds me of . . .
1. Alligators	1. Wolves (sharp teeth)
2. Cold-blooded animals (frogs and snakes)	2. Amazon river

Concept or topic: Crocodiles

In my life . . .	Picture or diagram:
1. Saw one at the zoo	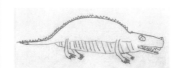
2. Saw one on the TV show, *River Monsters*	
3. Went to gator farm in Florida	

- **Brainstorm and Confirm.** This can be done in a large or small group, pairs, or individually. Before reading, students brainstorm what they know about the text topic. Brainstormed ideas should be recorded. As they read, students use a pencil and put a checkmark (✓) in the margin of the text every time they encounter a brainstormed idea. You can make this into a game format by putting students in small groups. Give them three minutes to brainstorm the things they know about the text topic. Again, put a ✓ in the margin of the text for every brainstormed idea. The group with the most checks is the winner.

- **Mind Pictures.** This is based on an idea described by Maureen McLaughlin in *Content Area Reading* (2010). At designated spots in the text, direct students to stop and create a picture, diagram, or some sort of visual representation of an idea from the text. This can be done individually or in pairs. Students can record their mind pictures in a journal or learning log, or create wall posters.

Last Word

This chapter describes strategies related to helping students comprehend expository text. The following teacher pre-reading strategies were described:

- List, group, and map
- Outlines
- Semantic maps and concept maps
- Guided notes
- What's my topic?

The following study-skill strategies were described:

- 5-step basic note-taking strategy
- Read, dot, and record
- Preview-overview
- Read and pause
- Paragraph reread
- 3 × 5 card
- Skim, reread, and note

And the following strategies used to develop cognitive processes were described:

- 3-I chart
- 3-I look back
- Double look back
- Reciprocal reading
- 3-I pre-post
- Preview and predict
- Connections
- Brainstorm and confirm
- Mind pictures

The last element to include would be practice. Students need to practice reading expository text. Try to find things besides textbooks here. I would recommend looking for short newspaper or magazine articles and webpages that are of interest to your students.

15

Vocabulary

> *Students learn the vast majority of new words naturally, by encountering them in meaningful contexts. We can enhance word learning by providing meaningful contexts that are rich in words.*

ATTENDING TO VOCABULARY

There are four reasons why attending to students' vocabulary is important. First, vocabulary knowledge enhances the development of students' emergent reading skills (Lane & Allen, 2010). Second, word knowledge enhances reading fluency and comprehension (Bauman, 2009; Blachowicz & Fisher, 2006; Jennings, Caldwell, & Lerner, 2010; Lipson & Wixon, 2009; Stahl, 1999). Third, vocabulary is strongly associated with concept learning (Blachowicz & Fisher, 2000). And fourth, words help us think (Stahl, 1999); they are tools of thought used to represent, manipulate, and extend our thinking (Vygotsky, 1962).

Word Learning

Children learn between 3,000 and 4,000 words a year (Anderson & Nagy, 1992; Graves & Silverman, 2011). By the end of elementary school they know approximately 25,000 and by the end of high school approximately 50,000 to 80,000 words (Harp & Brewer, 2005). The question is this: How do they learn all these words? Do they learn them from vocabulary worksheets? Do they learn them by looking them up and writing down the definition? Do they learn them as a result of direct instruction? Let's do the math. We will use the more conservative estimate of 3,000 words each year. The average school year consists of about 180 days. If each of these days were an instructional day, this would mean children would need to have a vocabulary worksheet with 17 new words on them each day. They would have to learn 85 new words a week or 340 words a month. That's a lot of vocabulary worksheets, dictionary activities, and direct instruction. It does not seem even remotely feasible that children can effectively learn new words this way.

So how do children learn new words? Take a minute to consider how it is that we as adults learn new words. *Twerking* is one of the myriad of new words that have slipped into our cultural lexicon. I first heard this word on some TV show in reference to Miley Cyrus. I got the sense that it had to do with something sexual. I picked this up from the context in which the word was used. I had only a sense of what it was about but could not have given you a definition until I looked it up on the Internet (I did it just for this chapter). Being a middle-aged man who is largely out of touch with popular media, I did not encounter this word often, and I certainly did not have opportunities to use it before writing this very paragraph.

In the same way, I first encountered the word "plethora" from watching the 1986 movie ¡*Three Amigos!*. This word was salient because I thought the scene in which it appeared was hilarious. Once aware of this word, I encountered it many times over the years until I eventually understood the many dimensions of the word. This word became easily recognized and eventually I could generate my own sentences using this word. At this point, it was firmly ensconced in my personal lexicon.

The big point is this: We learn the vast majority of our words naturally, by encountering them in meaningful contexts (Bauman, 2009; Lipson & Wixson, 2009; Rasinski, Padak, & Fawett, 2010). Throughout our lives, we continue to learn new words this way (Blachowicz & Fisher, 2006; Lane & Allen, 2010). Consider the seven words in Figure 15.1. I would posit that most would not be able to offer a precise definition of most of these. Yet, simply by encountering them in the previous text, you probably have a general sense of what each word means. This is because they were encountered in meaningful contexts.

This illustrates how we learn new words. And an even bigger point is this: The more words we encounter in meaningful contexts, the more words we learn (Lane & Allen, 2010). Thus, the best and most effective way to improve students' vocabulary is through wide reading (Bauman, 2009; Blachowicz & Fisher, 2000; Jennings, Caldwell, & Lerner, 2010; Krashen, 2004; Rasinski, Padak, & Fawett, 2010).

Figure 15.1   Interesting or Important Words

myriad, lexicon, twerking, plethora, salient, ensconce, posit

Levels and Types of Word Knowledge

As mentioned above, we know words at varying levels. At the lowest level, we have a sense of what a word might be related to. At the next level, we understand a word when it is seen or heard in the context of a sentence. At the highest level, we fully understand the word in all dimensions, we can generate our own definitions, and we can use the word in many contexts. These levels of word knowledge help us understand four different types of vocabularies.

Our *listening vocabulary* consists of the words that we hear and understand in conversations. Our *speaking vocabulary* consists of the words we use in formal and information conversations. We understand more words in context than we are able to use. Our *reading vocabulary* consists of the words we are able to recognize as we read. Most children enter school with very few words in their reading vocabulary. As they develop word identification skills, this number increases rapidly. To the greatest extent possible, the words that emergent and beginning readers encounter in text should be words that they already know. Our *writing vocabulary* consists of the words we use to express ourselves in written form. This is smaller than our reading vocabulary. However, once we have fully developed our word identification skills, our receiving vocabularies (listening and reading) are fairly similar, as are our transmission vocabularies (speaking and writing).

Volume and Vocabulary

The amount of reading that students do has a positive impact on all areas of reading as well as vocabulary (Bauman, 2009; Cunningham

& Stanovich, 2001; Jennings, Caldwell, & Lerner, 2010; Krashen, 2011). The data in Figure 15.2 is from a study conducted by Anderson, Wilson, and Fielding (1988). It shows how profound the differences are in the achievement levels, time spent reading independently, and words encountered each year. What is most significant are the differences in the numbers of words encountered. While correlation does not infer causation, it is safe to suggest that those who read more will encounter more words and become better readers. Those who read less will encounter fewer words and will not develop their reading skills as quickly.

Figure 15.2   Variation in the Amount of Independent Reading

Percentile Ranking—Reading Achievement	Independent Reading—Minutes per Day	Words Read per Year
98	65.0	4,358,000
90	21.1	1,823,000
80	14.2	1,146,000
70	9.6	6,222,000
60	6.5	432,000
50	4.6	22,000
40	3.2	200,000
30	1.3	106,000
20	0.7	21,000
10	0.1	8,000
2	0	0

GENERAL PRINCIPLES FOR DEVELOPING STUDENTS' VOCABULARY

While effective vocabulary "instruction" has some elements of formal instruction, it should primarily build upon how we naturally learn new words. In this sense, we don't teach vocabulary; rather, we create the conditions that enable students to develop their knowledge of words. Described below are seven general principles to guide you here. The section that follows includes descriptions of specific strategies built on these principles.

1. Promote wide reading. It should be more than a little obvious by now that wide reading is the most effective way to learn new words (Bauman, 2009; Krashen, 2004). Setting aside 10 to 20 minutes a day for silent, sustained, self-selected reading (SSSR) is a simple, effective, inexpensive, research-based strategy that can be used in all settings and at all levels. Wide reading includes teacher read alouds (Bauman, 2009). Reading aloud to students every day (even for 5 minutes) has many benefits, including exposing students to new words, modeling syntax and sentence structure, and introducing students to a variety of authors and genre.

2. Model sophisticated word usage. Teacher modeling of new words enables students to learn new words incidentally in authentic contexts as well as develop word consciousness. Simply becoming aware of the words you use and trying to infuse more sophisticated words into your classroom language can also be helpful in enhancing students' vocabulary. One related activity (Purposefully Planned Vocabulary Infusion) is described below.

3. Provide contextual and definitional information. When new words are introduced, provide both contextual and definitional information. This means students should always see or hear a new word in the context of a sentence. First, ask students to use contextual information to make a reasoned guess. Then, provide a definition using what I call *kid language*. Kid language means that you use words and concepts that are within students' experiences. It does little good to provide a dictionary definition if that definition includes more unfamiliar words and concepts.

4. Connect new to the known. When introducing a new word (or concept), always try to link new words to known words and concepts (Jennings, Caldwell, & Learner, 2010).

5. Provide multiple exposures. An initial exposure does very little to move a new word into students' vocabulary. Students need to encounter new words many times in a variety of contexts over time.

6. Promote active, in-depth processing of words. New words can be learned deeply by employing activities that involve active processing (Bauman, 2009; Lipson & Wixson, 2009). There are three levels of active processing. The *associative level* is where students make connections between one word and another through synonyms and association. The *comprehension level* is where students demonstrate their understanding of a word. This can be done by categorizing words or sets of words, filling in a deleted word from a sentence, or connecting a word with the correct definition. The *generational level* is where students use a word in new ways. Here students provide a definition using their own words or use the word in authentic writing or speaking activities.

7. Connect word learning to concept learning. One of the best occasions for addressing vocabulary is when learning new concepts in science, social studies, or other curriculum areas. When teaching new concepts, introduce vocabulary using diagrams, semantic maps, or other forms of graphic organizers that enable students to perceive the relatedness and interrelatedness of the new words and concept (see below).

STRATEGIES FOR DEVELOPING STUDENTS' VOCABULARY

Based on the seven principles described above, specific strategies for developing students' vocabulary are presented here:

1. Purposefully Planned Vocabulary Infusion. Purposefully planned vocabulary infusion (PPVI), is based on a strategy described by Lane and Allen (2010). Here the teacher embeds and models sophisticated vocabulary during instruction and daily conversation with students. To do this, first, identify words that are used in general classroom conversation or instruction. Then, find more sophisticated versions of these words or related words. For example, instead of gather, you might insert the word *congregate* to say, "Can we congregate at the front please?" Next, plan places in which to purposefully substitute the target word each day. Finally, keep a tally of when and where you model the word. I would recommend that you start by introducing four to six new words each week. You can also identify words related to specific areas of the curriculum (science, social studies, reading, health, etc.), and make purposeful placement of these words. PPVI can be enhanced by including any of the other strategies described below.

2. Etymology Minilessons. Here, a very brief bit of instruction related to the origin of a word or the meaning of a root word is provided. Here is an example: Congregate means to come together or assemble. Two related words are congregation and congress. Congregation is a group that comes together at a church. Congress is a group of lawmakers that come together in Washington DC. There are a variety of free etymology dictionaries on the Internet (www .etymonline.com). Etymology minilessons should be brief and visual. When possible, use a graphic organizer to show related words, word parts, and varying forms of the target word (below).

   3. Word Walls, Visual Displays, and Graphic Organizers. Use word walls (described in Chapter 10) and other types of graphic organizers to display new words. These should be used for instruction initially, then displayed for review and continued reference. A variety of different graphic organizers and visual displays are described below.

   4. Synonyms and Associations (SA). SA is a strategy designed to add depth and dimension to word knowledge. This can be done as a whole-class activity initially, but it works best as a small-group activity as it invites conversation and processing at deeper levels. Use a graphic organizer similar to Figure 15.3 when doing an SA activity.

   The steps are as follows: First, provide the target word in the context of a sentence or sentences. Second, invite students to make inferences as to the possible meaning of the word. Third, provide a definition using kid language. Fourth, invite students to find synonymous words and phrases and write these in the first column. You may have to teach students how to use the synonyms function of their word processor or to use an online thesaurus for this step. (For students at the emergent level who may have trouble with this step, list five to six synonyms, and ask them to select three that they think are

Figure 15.3   Synonyms and Associations

The football player was very **aggressive**. He ran hard and fast.	
Aggressive: Doing something forcefully or with strong energy.	
Synonyms	**Associations**
violent	MMA fighters
hostile	tornados
hard action	hungry tigers
forceful	angry arguments
belligerent	pushing and shoving
strongly assertive	rushing to the front of the line
forward	bullies
angry energy	
combative—willing to fight	

most interesting or important.) Finally, ask students to list things or experiences they associate with the target word. The graphic organizers should be displayed on a bulletin board or word wall. They can be augmented with pictures or diagrams. A simplified version of the SA chart for younger students is in Figure 15.4.

Figure 15.4   A Simplified SA Chart

Mary is very **inquisitive.**

Synonyms	Associations—Makes you think about . . .
curious snoopy asking questions wants to know nosey	• wrapped birthday presents • a good mystery • a detective • none of your business • gossip • a really interesting class

Synonym Box

curious, snoopy, asks lots of questions, wants to know, nosey, prying, meddling, intrusive, inquisitive, interested, questioning

A slightly different variation of the SA chart is the Super Word Web (SWW) (Johnson, 2008). Here, you again introduce the word, either orally or in writing, in the context of a sentence (see Figure 15.5). A definition is provided by the teacher or, when working in small group, a dictionary. Synonymous words and phrases are listed inside the box. Associations are then listed along the outside of the box. Students can create their SWW on butcher paper for display in the classroom or in their reading logs or learning journals. Encourage students to be creative in the shape of the word box used to list synonyms. For example, if the word was an automobile word, the synonyms could be put inside the shape of a car. Also, encourage students to draw pictures of their associations. In this way, you bring multiple modes of thinking and visual references to the study of words.

5. SA as Pre-Reading Activity. SA can be used as a pre-reading activity. Here you assign each small group a different word related to the upcoming text. Students complete the SA graphic organizers (see Figure 15.3) and display them on a wall or bulletin board. You can

Figure 15.5   Super Word Web

Steps

1. See the word in context.

2. List three or four synonyms or defining phrases inside the figure.

3. List or draw three or four associations.

4. Use in pairs or small groups—create a poster or journal entry.

EXAMPLE: *myriad*

EXAMPLE: He had a *myriad* of things to do.

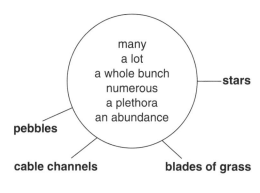

extend this by asking students to make predictions, based on the word clues, as to what they think the topic of the assigned reading might be.

6. Interesting Words or Word Usage. Create an interest in words by recognizing interesting words or word usage encountered in text or other places. Ask students to be on the lookout for these as well. Song lyrics, movies, and television can be rich in interesting words and word usages. Have a place on a bulletin board or word wall for recording and displaying these. You can use a word box similar to one of those in Figure 15.6.

7. Parallel Personal Writing Prompts. Simply asking students to write a sentence using the new word can often result in an abstract, meaningless sentence. However, a parallel personal writing prompt is one that gets students using the new word in the context of their own lives or experiences. For example, Mr. Jay was introducing the word "onus." To get his sixth-grade students to use this word he created a

Figure 15.6 Word Box

Word	Sentence	Meaning
congregate	The villains were congregating down by the river.	Meet or gather
myriad	Sally had a myriad of choices from which to choose.	Many, a whole bunch

parallel personal writing prompt that asked them to describe something for which they are responsible in their lives. They were asked to finish the sentence, "In my life, the onus is on me to . . ." Then he said, "Now tell me more about this. Why is this important? Do you enjoy it? What would happen if you didn't do it?"

8. **Connection.** This small-group activity is designed to add depth and dimension to students' current word knowledge. It can be used as a pre-/post-reading activity. Before reading the assigned text, give students two lists of words. The first list contains the key vocabulary words found in the text or lesson (see Figure 15.7). The second contains a list of words that are related in some way to a word from the first list. In small group, students connect the words and state their reasons for making the connection. As a post-reading activity, students go back and make necessary revisions.

Figure 15.7 Connection Activity

Column A	Column B
MYRIAD	blood
PLASMA	blow up or explode
CARCINOMA	burn, start on fire
CARCINOGENIC	many
FLAMMABLE	poisonous
COMBUSTION	skin cancer

9. **Word Sort.** This activity is also used to add depth and dimension to existing word knowledge and build upon students' current knowledge base. It can also be used as a pre-/post-reading activity.

First, develop a list of important words related to the assigned reading. The words should be written on 3 × 5 cards for younger children so they can physically manipulate them. For older children, the words can simply be displayed. In small group, ask students to put the words into groups or categories related to meaning as a pre-reading or lesson activity. A group is two or more things that have something that makes them the same. Finally, ask students to create a name or label for each group. As a post-reading or lesson activity ask students to make necessary corrections.

10. Classifying. This works best using words with which students have had some exposure. Here students are given two or more new target words which are used as category headings. They are also given a variety of related words that are either synonymous or associated with one of the new target words (see Figure 15.8). Students have

Figure 15.8   Classifying Words

Classifying for Emergent-Level Readers

run	jump	sleep

race, bed, dart, slumber, dash, leap, spring, skip, nap, snooze

Classifying for Beginning-Level Readers and Above

eat	sit	roll	jump	run	hunt	sleep
feed	rest	turn	leap	race	stalk	dose
dine	take a seat	whirl	spring	dash	look for	nap
swallow		spin	skip	dart		snooze
munch	perch				chase	slumber
	settle					

feed, nap, snooze, slumber, dine, swallow, race, dash, dart, stalk, look for, chase, munch, rest, take a seat, spring, skip, turn, whirl, perch, settle, spin, leap, dose to find the right target-word category for each of the related words. Again, with younger children it works best if they can physically manipulate words using 3 × 5 word cards. Having students work in pairs or small groups creates important learning discussions. Creating a poster or bulletin board display will enable you to use this for future reference and other word-related activities.

11. Vocabulary Rating. Vocabulary rating is best used as a pre-post-reading activity. Before the assigned reading, show students the target words and ask them to rate their level of word knowledge (Figure 15.9). After the assigned reading or lesson, ask them to again rate their level of word knowledge. This works effectively as a small group activity. Here you would ask the group to rate its knowledge of the word. The conversation that takes place within the group around the words serves to enhance understanding. Vocabulary rating charts like this can also be adapted for use at various points during the year to assess students' general word knowledge.

Figure 15.9   Vocabulary-Rating Chart

Levels of Word Knowledge →	1 = never seen/heard it
	2 = have seen/heard it
	3 = know what it's about
	4 = understand it
	5 = can use and define it

	Pre-	Post-
arch		
decorate		
fossils		
graphite		
jewelry		
mountains		
statues		
plebiscite		

12. Semantic-Features Analysis. This activity also invites students to add depth and dimension to their word knowledge. It is ideal for expository text or when teaching concepts. Create a table in which target words are listed in the vertical column on the far left (see Figure 15.10). List a set of descriptors or semantic features along the horizontal axis at the top. As the words are encountered in the text, students check the semantic features that apply. This can also be done as a pre-post-reading activity in pairs or small groups. Again, the conversation that takes place is an essential component here.

Figure 15.10   Semantic Features Analysis

	It is alive.	I've seen one.	It is big.	It is a describing word.	It is an action word.	It goes fast.
cheetah	×					×
plane		×	×			×
tortoise	×	×				
train		×	×			×
skyrocket			×			×
fast				×		
transfer					×	
sluggishly				×		
flies					×	

VISUAL DISPLAYS AND GRAPHIC ORGANIZERS

This last section describes a variety of visual displays and graphic organizers. They can be used as teaching devices. They can also be displayed on a wall or bulletin board for easy reference, revisiting, and review. As well, students can create their own visual displays or graphic organizers for posters or bulletin board displays or for their learning logs. Finally, the words here can be used for quick games, riddles, or sponge activities.

1. Synonyms. Figure 15.11 shows the target word in the context of a sentence, uses kid language to define the word, and provides a list of synonymous words and phrases. One way to keep these relevant is to put these at a level at which students have access, and include a pencil or marker. Then, encourage students to add their own words, concepts, or pictures underneath each target word.

Figure 15.11 Synonyms

Aggressive: Doing something forcefully or with strong energy.	**Congregate:** Come together or gather.
He was **aggressive**.	Please **congregate** at the front of the room.
violent, hostile, forceful, belligerent, strongly assertive, forward, angry energy, combative —willing to fight	assemble, convene, rendezvous, cluster, meet, group, assemble, gather

2. Related Word Forms. After an etymology minilesson, post related word forms so that students can see the relationship between words. Figure 15.12 is in map form. Figure 15.13 is in list form and includes forms of the words. Use both.

Figure 15.12 Related Words

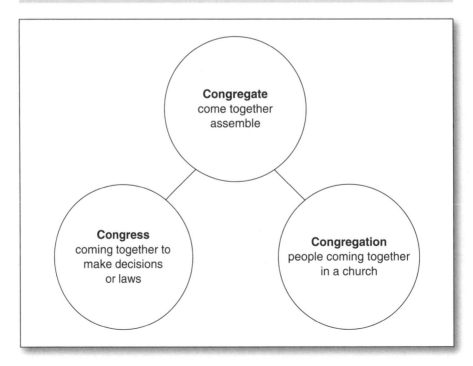

Figure 15.13 Related Word Forms With Forms of Words

Congregate: come together, assemble	Congress: coming together to make decisions or laws	Congregation: people coming together In a church
congregating congregated	congressional congressman congresswoman congressperson congressing congressed	congregational congregations

3. Conceptually Related Words. These are words related to a particular concept you are teaching or reading about (e.g., rain, weather, sleet, evaporation, water cycle, etc.) or words arranged in categories around a particular theme or story (see Figure 15.14). This provides a context for seeing new words and presents a visual reference for reviewing ideas covered in previous lessons.

Figure 15.14 Conceptually Related Word Displays

blood
transfusion
hemoglobin
blood cells
plasma
circulation
oxygen
heart

4. Semantic Maps and Concept Maps. These were described in Chapter 14. Both can be used to put new words in a meaningful context for initial learning and then posted for reference, revisiting, and review. To use as a post-reading activity present just the map without any words in them. Use a word box to display the target words. Have students work in pairs or small groups to arrange and insert the target words on the map.

5. Diagrams. Display posters or diagrams that include labels or new vocabulary.

6. Vocabulary Maps. Sometimes known as word maps or definition maps, these come in many forms. However, the salient elements include a target word, a definition, properties or descriptors, and some examples. Other elements that can be included are pictures, related words, a sentence containing the word, synonyms, and comparisons to known things. Figure 15.15 shows six examples. Adopt and adapt.

Figure 15.15 Vocabulary Maps

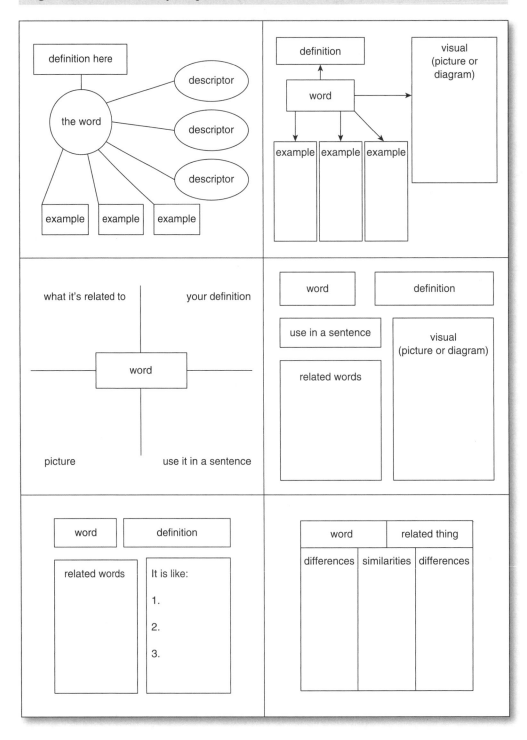

Last Word About Words

Word knowledge affects students' ability to learn and comprehend what they read. The goals of effective vocabulary instruction are to expand students' vocabularies, strengthen their depth and dimension of word knowledge, and move new words into their productive vocabulary. To this end, the following strategies were described:

- Purposefully planned vocabulary infusion (PPVI)
- Etymology minilessons
- Word walls, visual displays, and graphic organizers
- Synonyms and associations (SA)
- SA as a pre-reading activity
- Interesting words or word usage
- Parallel personal writing prompts
- Connection
- Word sort
- Classifying
- Vocabulary rating
- Semantic features analysis

This chapter also examined different ways to display new vocabulary words. The following were described:

- Synonyms
- Related word forms
- Conceptually related words
- Semantic maps and concept maps
- Diagrams
- Vocabulary maps

We learn the vast majority of new words naturally, by encountering them in meaningful contexts. Wide reading is one of the best and most efficient ways to encounter a large number of words. The strategies described in this chapter are most effective when used in conjunction with programs designed to promote wide reading.

16

Writing

> *When working with struggling writers, it is important to find the structure necessary to enable them to engage in authentic writing activities without frustration.*

I want to be very clear about one thing: The purpose of this chapter is NOT to demonstrate how to teach students to write. That will come in another book. The purpose of this chapter is to describe strategies for using writing to enhance students' ability to read.

THE WHY AND HOW OF WRITING

After wide reading, writing is probably the next best thing you can use to help struggling readers. You often hear beginning and emergent readers sounding out words as they listen to find the correct letter sounds during writing activities. This helps in the development of the phonetic cueing system. Writing also invites students to focus on word order, grammar, and the logical structure of the language, all elements that comprise the syntactical-cueing system.

10 General Guidelines

Many struggling readers have a strong aversion to writing. Why? Because they can't do it very well. Keeping this in mind, below are 10 general guidelines for working with students who may struggle with writing:

1. Don't frustrate your students. Getting words on the page can be very difficult for struggling writers. Simply asking them to write without providing support will only frustrate them. Instead, provide scaffolding to enable students to successfully engage in authentic writing activities. (The strategies presented in this chapter will help here.) Scaffolding helps students to develop a sense of self-efficacy and eliminates many of the strong negative emotions associated with writing.

2. Teach and model the writing process. Specifically teach and model all five stages of the writing process: (a) generating ideas, (b) drafting, (c) revising, (d) editing, and (e) sharing.

3. Always celebrate ideas first. Writing is used to record and transmit ideas. Thus, writing should always be a celebration of ideas. Spelling, grammar, and punctuation are important because they enable us to accurately express ideas. Focus on these only during the editing stage.

4. Use temporary spelling. Worrying about spelling while generating ideas and making word choices can make writing overwhelming for some students. If students pause because they can't spell a word during the drafting or revising stages, tell them, "Don't worry about the spelling right now. Just use enough letters to hold the idea. We'll look at spelling at the end."

5. Use self-selected spelling tests. Weekly spelling tests do very little to enhance students' ability to spell under real-life writing conditions (Graves, 1983). If you must give spelling tests, I recommend allowing students to choose five to ten words that they want to study each week (Johnson, 1998). You can still include two to five mandatory words. Each student would have his or her personal spelling test. During the week you would create activities that would get students to use their words. When it comes time to give the spelling test, students hand their personalized list to a classmate who then administers it.

6. Write for real life audiences whenever possible. Writing becomes alive when other people read and respond to it. Figure 16.1

contains some simple ideas to get students to read and respond to each other's writing.

Figure 16.1 Ways for Students to Share Their Writing

1. **Turn to a neighbor.** After a writing session, have students share all or part of their writing with a neighbor. Give struggling writers the option of reading or simply telling about their writing.
2. **Trade with a neighbor**. After you have developed trust within a classroom, have students trade papers with a classmate.
3. **Share in small group.** Depending on the age, have students move into groups of three to five to read their writing.
4. **Post on a blog or Internet site.** Create a website or blog for students to post and respond to each other's writing. (Make sure you talk about Internet etiquette first.)
5. **Create books (online or paper).** Students love to read the writing of other students. Use the students' writing to create books.
6. **Display writing.** Use the wall or bulletin board to display interesting or unique writing. (Always ask students for permission before displaying their writing.)
7. **Author's chair.** Have one to two students sign up to share their writing with the whole class each day. (I recommend no more than three students a day.)

7. Teach students how to respond to each other's writing. Use the four prompts in Figure 16.2 to teach students how to respond to the ideas of others. Post these in a place where all can see them. Students will rely on these prompts initially but will eventually be able to respond without them.

Figure 16.2 Responding to Writing

Responding to Our Friends' Writing

1. I like . . .
2. It reminds me of . . .
3. I don't understand . . .
4. I want to know more about . . .

8. Help students with writing topics initially. Students need to be able to write using their own writing topics. However, this may be difficult initially, especially with students who have a strong aversion to writing. You can help by conducting brainstorming sessions for writing topic ideas with students. Have them record and keep this list in their journal or writing log.

9. Rarely ask students for more. If students finish writing about a topic and they have written very little, avoid the temptation to ask them to go back and write more. In most cases, students have said all that they wanted to say. Asking them to write more will result in more words on the page but not better writing. Quality is not the same as quantity. If you want more writing, have them find something else to write about. More complex and sophisticated writing will occur naturally as a result of the responses students get from you and others and as they read and respond to the writing of others.

10. Write with your students. Teachers of writing need to write and share their writing with students. Students love to hear your authentic voice and experiences. Also, doing your own writing enables you to teach and model the writing process using your own writing. Example: "When I was writing this paragraph it didn't sound right, so I read it out loud a couple of times and heard some things that didn't need to be there."

SPECIFIC STRATEGIES

Chapter 11 described four strategies for using writing to help develop students' syntactic-cueing system (syntax sentences, sentence combing, sentence alteration, and sentence elaboration). Below are 13 additional strategies. These are all very simple strategies designed to be used within the context of reading instruction. Again, the purpose of this chapter is not to provide direction on teaching writing; rather, it is to describe strategies for using writing to help students' reading.

• **Sentence Mix Up**. This strategy was described for developing the syntactic-cueing system. This is also a form of writing at a very basic level. Here, students see the sentence and are given 3 × 5 cards with each word in the sentence on it. The words are mixed up and students have to put them in order. To extend this, present the sentence orally and have students put the cards back in order. At the highest level, give students the words without any prompts and ask them to put them in order in a way that makes sense. This last variation works well in pairs or groups of three. This can also be used as a postreading activity by making the sentences directly related to what students have read.

• **Predictable Writing.** This was described briefly in Chapter 7. It works best for students at the emergent level. There are two ways you can use predictable writing: First, write three or four sentences with one word missing for use with individual students (see Figure 16.3). For example "I like to _____." Students then fill in the blank telling you about three things they like to do. Second, create a large poster and have each student in your class fill in one line. When you're done, students reread the sentences until fluent.

Figure 16.3   Predictable Writing

Things I Like to Do

I like to _____.

I like to _____.

I like to _____.

I like to _____.

• **One Sentence.** With students who are struggling writers, start by asking them to write one sentence. This keeps them from being overwhelmed. Initially, you might need to help students identify what they want to say. Look for a sentence that is of relevance to them by asking questions to solicit ideas (Figure 16.4). If a student says, "I don't know" (which happens frequently in the beginning stages) say, "Okay. Let's write that. 'I don't know what to say.'"

Have students speak the sentence before writing. Make sure it is a complete sentence. For example, if the student says something like, "At the park." Ask the question, "If you walked up to somebody and said, 'At the park,' would that person know what you were talking about?" This helps the writer develop a sense of audience as well as complete sentences.

Break long, run-on sentences into short sentences. The student might say something like, "Yesterday we went to my Grandpa's house

Figure 16.4   Questions to Elicit One-Sentence Writing

1. What do you want to say today?

2. What did you do that was fun yesterday?

3. What did you see on your way to school?

4. What's something you like to do?

5. What are you going to do this weekend?

6. What are you thinking about?

7. What are you going to do at recess?

8. What are you thinking about right now?

and went swimming at the lake and it was really, really fun because my cousins were there." This is where you edit using short sentences whenever possible. "We were at Grandpa's house. My cousins were there. We went swimming. It was fun."

- **Priming Pictures.** Sometimes it's easier for students to describe a picture. Look for a fun, interesting, unique, or relevant pictures on the Internet. If possible, use pictures that include subjects about the same age as your students. Copy and paste these in students' computer journals, on a sheet of paper, or project them onto a screen. To extend, ask older students to take their own pictures (cellphones or cameras) to bring in and describe.

- **Scaffolded Writing Using a Keyboard.** Use this with students who are struggling to write one or two sentences using a keyboard. As the student writes, provide very quiet verbal clues to help the student hear each part of the word. As the student finishes each word, repeat the sentence. This frees up working memory for students to focus on word order and meaning. Also, help the student find the letter keys on the keyboard by pointing to the general area where the keys are. Again, this enables the student to focus on meaning without spending valuable cognitive resources looking for keys. When finished, the student should reread sentences until fluency is achieved.

- **Assisted Writing Using Paper.** Use this with students who are struggling to write one or two sentences on paper. The student should write one sentence at a time, skipping every other line. If the student is unsure of how to spell a word, tell the student to use a letter or two to hold the idea. Once the sentence is completed, ask the student if there are any words that don't look right. (Students are usually able to identify all of these.) Once identified, cross out the word and write the correct spelling on top of it. The student writes the correct spelling beneath the word. When the sentences are completed, the student reads through the sentences until fluency is achieved (usually two or three times). If you are working in small groups, students should work with a partner to identify words that don't look right. Teach them how to use spellcheck programs.

 • **Template Writing.** This works best for students in the intermediate grades and above. Here you choose from a menu of sentences to create a template for writing a short paragraph. Figure 16.5 has a menu of sentences that can be used for template writing. Post these on a board or wall. Use two or three sentence each day. Eventually, students can choose their own sentences for their journal. You might say something like, "Use any three sentences for your journal writing today." Eventually, students will be able to write without using template sentences.

Figure 16.5   Menus of Sentences for Template Writing

1. My name is _____.

2. I like to _____.

3. I don't like to _____.

4. Someday I hope to _____.

5. I really like it when _____.

6. ____ drives me crazy.

7. Tomorrow I will _____.

8. This week I will _____.

9. ____ makes me happy.

10. I can _____.

11. I am very good at _____.

12. When I get older I will _____.

13. Now that I am older I must _____.

14. My favorite ____ is _____.

15. I don't like _____.

16. I will work with ____ to _____.

17. My goal this week is to _____.

18. I want to remember to _____.

19. Tomorrow I have to _____.

20. ____ is _____.

21. ____ is the person I would like to____ with.

22. Today is _____.

23. I like it when _____.

24. It was fun. We _____.

25. I had fun. I _____.

26. I remember when _____.

27. I wish that _____.

28. I wish I could _____.

29. I would like to be able to _____.

30. ____makes me feel _____.

31. It was scary when _____.

32. When I am bored I _____.

33. I really had fun when _____.

34. ____is very_____.

35. I could believe it when _____.

36. I am proud of _____.

37. I get angry when _____.

38. When I'm feeling sad I _____.

39. On the way to school I saw _____.

40. I saw _____.

41. I really like to _____.

42. I just don't understand _____.

43. I don't understand it when _____.

44. Sometimes I wish my friends would _____.

45. Sometimes I wish _____ would _____.

46. _____ is somebody I admire.

47. I would like to be _____.

48. I would like to be like _____.

49. It was _____ when _____.

50. _____ makes me feel _____.

51. ____is a good friend. We like to _____.

• **Facilitated Writing.** Facilitated writing can be done individually or in a small group. Again, start by using just one sentence. Ask students what they want to say. As they tell you, write down just the "big" words on the screen or board. For example, if a student said, "The football game was incredible." You would write, "football, game, incredible," on the board, screen, or paper for them to see. Here you are creating a word box for students to use for writing. This provides structure for students to successfully write the sentence. Move from one or two sentences to a paragraph.

• **Dictated Sentences.** It is appropriate at times to dictate sentences to students. I recommend using no more than one or two sentences at a time here. You can use these sentences to reinforce letter sounds, common phonograms, and sight words. Try to make the sentences relevant to students' lives and include some open-ended sentences (see Figure 16.6). To extend this, write four to six words from the most frequent word poster on the board and ask students to create their own sentences.

• **Texting Practice.** Older students often have to be told to stop texting in school. However, texting can be a very immediate way to practice an authentic form of reading and writing. Using a sheet of paper with large squares on it (see Figure 16.7), have students sit next to a classmate and practice a texting conversation. They cannot talk;

Figure 16.6   Examples of Sentence Dictation
Using Most Frequent Words

1. I am very _____.
2. They are in the lake.
3. We are in here.
4. I like it when _____.
5. I will do my work, then I will go home.
6. I would like to know more about you.
7. Can you please come here?
8. How many candy bars can you eat?
9. I see that there are many cats.
10. I do not know her.

Figure 16.7   Texting Practice

rather, they have to pass the paper back and forth using the squares as their texting screen. Students can help you create a poster of common texting abbreviations for use in their texting conversations.

- **Speech-to-Text Software**. Speech-to-text software programs are widely available today. As the student speaks, the words appear on the computer screen. They are not always accurate, but this provides editing opportunities. The best programs have a playback function where the computer reads what the student has written (see below).

• **Text-to-Speech Software.** Equally helpful is the text-to-speech software. When a letter is pressed, it makes the letter sound. When a word is complete, it will read the word back or the sentence back. This makes writing more concrete and real for students who are struggling writers.

• **Support-A-Statement.** This strategy helps students learn how to write paragraphs by identifying a statement and supporting ideas. First, identify a topic statement. This could come from a book as a post-reading activity or from students' lives (see Figure 16.8). Next, students list at least two ideas that support or are related to that statement. Use the graphic organizer in Figure 16.9. Don't worry about

Figure 16.8   Topic Statements for Support-A-Statement

1. _____ is wonderful.

2. _____ is not wonderful.

3. _____ is exciting.

4. _____ is not exciting.

5. I really like _____.

6. I really don't like _____.

7. I would like to _____.

8. I would not like to _____.

9. I would like to learn more about _____.

10. I am not interested in learning about _____.

11. Someday I hope to _____.

12. I hope I never have to _____.

13. I get nervous when _____.

14. I am relaxed when _____.

15. I really enjoy _____.

16. I do not enjoy _____.

17. My favorite part of school is _____.

18. On weekends I like to _____.

19. On weekends I don't like to _____.

20. I love it when _____.

21. I hate it when _____.

22. _____ makes me excited.

23. _____ makes me feel bored.

24. I believe that _____.

25. I think that _____.

26. I feel strongly that _____.

27. I really hope that _____.

28. I want _____ to change (or be changed).

29. There should be a law that _____.

30. There should be a rule that _____.

Figure 16.9   Support-A-Statement Graphic Organizer

Topic Statement:

Supporting Ideas:

   1.

   2.

   3.

Paragraph:

students writing complete sentences at this stage. Tell them to use words to hold the idea. Then, students create a simple paragraph using the statement and supporting ideas. Finally, students read the paragraph out loud to make sure it sounds the way they want, and then check for spelling.

Last Word

The focus of this chapter was on how to use writing in the context of reading instruction. The following strategies were described:

- Sentence mix up
- Predictable writing
- One sentence
- Priming pictures
- Scaffolded writing using a keyboard
- Assisted writing using paper
- Template writing
- Facilitated writing
- Dictated sentences
- Texting practice
- Speech-to-text software
- Text-to-speech software
- Support-A-statement

All the strategies in this chapter have been thoroughly kid-tested with students from kindergarten to high school. Writing helps developing students' ability to create meaning with print. In working with struggling writers, you will need to find the structure and scaffolding necessary to enable them to engage in authentic writing activities without frustrating them.

Epilogue

Well, there you have it then. This book has come to an end. Hopefully you understand the process of reading a little better and you have some new strategies to use with struggling readers. My next book will focus on helping struggling writers and will be out soon. Until then, I will leave you with eight simple rules for creating effective reading instruction.

1. Keep it simple.

2. Adopt and adapt.

3. Help students fall in love with books.

4. Read real things.

5. Write for authentic purposes.

6. Include as much choice as possible.

7. Keep instructional proximal (do not frustrate your students).

8. Address the 10 instructional elements in your curriculum.

Andy Johnson, PhD
andrew.axe.johnson@gmail.com
www.OPDT-Johnson.com

References

Alitto, H. J., & Usrey, W. M. (2003). Corticothalamic feedback and sensory processing. *Current Opinion in Neurobiology, 13,* 440–445.

Allington, R. (2005). *What really matters for struggling readers: Designing research-based programs* (2nd ed.). New York, NY: Longman.

Allington, R. (2012). *What really matters for struggling readers: Designing research-based programs.* Boston, MA: Pearson.

Allington, R. L., & McGill-Franzen, A. (2009). Comprehension difficulties among struggling readers. In S. Israel & G. Duffy (Eds.), *Handbook of research on reading comprehension* (pp. 551–568). New York, NY: Routledge.

Almasi, J. F., Palmer, B. M., Madden, A., & Hart, S. (2001). Interventions to enhance narrative comprehension. In A. McGill-Franzen & R. Allington (Eds.), *Handbook of reading disability research* (pp. 329–344). New York, NY: Routledge.

Anderson, R. (2013). Role of the reader's schema in comprehension, learning, and memory. In D. Alvermann, N. J. Unrau, & R. B. Ruddell (Eds.), *Theoretical models and processes of reading* (pp. 476–488). Newark, DE: International Reading Association.

Anderson, R. C., & Nagy, W. E. (1992). The vocabulary conundrum. *American Educator, 16*(4), 14–18, 44–47.

Anderson, R. C., Wilson, P. T., & Fielding, L. G. (1988). Growth in reading and how children spend their time outside of school. *Reading Research Quarterly, 23,* 285–303.

Andersson, B. V., & Barnitz, J. G. (1984). Cross-cultural schemata and reading comprehension instruction. *Journal of Reading,* 28, 102–108.

Atwell, N. (1998). *In the middle: New understandings about writing, reading, and learning* (2nd ed.). Portsmouth, NH: Boynton/Cook.

Baars, B. J., & Gage, N. M. (2007). *Cognition, brain and consciousness: Introduction to cognitive neuroscience.* New York, NY: Academic Press.

Bauman, J. F. (2009). Vocabulary and reading comprehension: The nexus of meaning. In S. E. Israel & G. G. Duffy (Eds.), *Handbook of Research on Reading Comprehension* (pp. 323–346). New York, NY: Routledge.

Bentum, K. E., & Aaron, P. G. (2003). Does reading instruction in learning disabilities resource rooms really work?: A longitudinal study. *Reading Psychology, 24,* 361–369.

Biemiller, A. (2006). Vocabulary development and instruction: A prerequisite for school learning. In D. K. Dickenson & S. B. Neuman (Eds.), *Handbook of early literacy research* (Vol. 2, pp. 41–51). New York, NY: Guildford Press.

Binder, K. S., Duffy, S. A., & Rayner, K. (2001). The effects of thematic fit and discourse context on syntactic ambiguity resolution. *Journal of Memory and Language, 44,* 297–324.

Blachowicz, C. L. Z., & Fisher, P. (2000). Vocabulary instruction. In R. Barr, M. L. Kamil, P. Mosenthal, & P. D. Pearsons (Eds.), *Handbook of reading research* (Vol. 3, pp. 503–523). Mahwah, NJ: Lawrence Erlbaum Associates.

Blachowicz, C. L. Z., & Fisher, P. (2006). *Teach vocabulary in all classrooms* (3rd ed.). Upper Saddle River, NH: Pearson Education.

Britto, P. R., Fuligni, A. S., & Brooks-Gunn, J. (2006). Reading ahead: Effective interventions for young children's early literacy development. In D. K. Dickenson & S. B. Neuman (Eds.), *Handbook of early literacy research* (Vol. 2, pp. 311–332). New York, NY: Guildford Press.

Cain, K., (2009). Making sense of text: Skills that support text comprehension and its development. *Perspectives on Language and Literacy, 35,* 11–14.

Caldwell, J. S., & Leslie, L. (2013). *Intervention strategies to follow informal reading inventory assessment: So what do I do now?* (3rd ed.) Boston, MA: Pearson.

Cambourne, B. (1993). *The whole story: Natural learning & the acquisition of literacy in the classroom.* New York, NY: Scholastic.

Casbergue, R. M., & McGee, L. (2011). Shifting perspectives in emergent literacy research. In A. McGill-Franzen & R. Allington (Eds.), *Handbook of reading disability research* (pp. 185–195). New York, NY: Routledge.

Chernove, G. V. (1979). Semantic aspects of psycholinguistic research in simultaneous interpretation. *Language and Speech, 22,* 277–295.

Chomsky, N. (1968). *Language and mind.* Orlando, FL: Harcourt, Brace & World.

Clay, M. M. (1982). *Observing young readers: Selected papers.* Exeter, NH: Heinemann.

Clay, M. M. (1991). *Becoming literate: The construction of inner control.* Portsmouth, NH: Heinemann.

Coles, G. (2003). *Reading the naked truth: Literacy, legislation, and lies.* Portsmouth, NH: Heinemann.

Cunningham, A. E., & Stanovich, K. E. (2001). What reading does for the mind. *Journal of Direct Instruction, 1,* 137–149.

Cunningham, P. M., & Allington, R. L. (2010). *Classrooms that work: They can all read and write* (5th ed.). Boston, MA: Pearson.

Cunningham, P. M., Hall, D. P., & Defee, M. (1998). Nonability-grouped, multilevel instruction: Eight years later. *The Reading Teacher, 51,* 652–664.

Destexhe, A. (2000). Modeling corticothalamic feedback and the gating of the thalamus by the cerebral corrects. *Journal of Physiology, 94,* 394–410.

Dickinson, D. K., McCabe, A., & Essex, M. J. (2006). A window of opportunity we must open to all: The case for preschool with high-quality support for language and literacy. In D. K. Dickenson & S. B. Neuman (Eds.), *Handbook of early literacy research* (Vol. 2, pp. 11–28). New York, NY: Guildford Press.

Dole, J. A., Nokes, J. D., & Drits, D. (2009). Cognitive strategy instruction. In S. Israel & G. Duffy (Eds.), *Handbook of research on reading comprehension* (pp. 347–373). New York, NY: Routledge.

Donnelly, N., & Davidoff, J. (1999). The mental representations of faces and houses: Issues concerning parts and wholes. *Visual Cognition, 6,* 319–343.

Ducket, P. (2008). Seeing the story for the words: The eye movements of beginning readers. In A. Flurky, E. Paulson, & K. Goodman (Eds.), *Scientific Realism in Studies of Reading* (pp. 113–128). New York, NY: Lawrence Erlbaum Associates.

Eggen, P., & Kauchak, D. (2007). *Educational psychology: Windows on classrooms* (7th ed.). Upper Saddle River, NJ: Pearson.

Engel, A. K., Fries, P., & Singer, W. (2001). Dynamic predictions: Oscillations and synchrony in top-down processing. *Nature Reviews Neuroscience, 2,* 704–716.

Erickson, K., Hanser, G., Hatch, P., & Sanders, E. (2009). *Research-based practices for creating access to the general curriculum in reading and literacy for students with significant intellectual disabilities.* Chapel Hill: University of North Carolina.

Erickson, K., & Koppenhaver, D. (2007). *Children with disabilities: Reading and writing the four-blocks way.* Greensboro, NC: Carson-Dellosa Publishing Company.

Fischer, K. W., Immordino-Yang, M. H., & Waber, D. (2007). Toward a grounded synthesis of mind, brain, and education for reading disorders: An introduction to the field and this book. In K. Fischer, J. H. Bernstein, & M. H. Immordino-Yang (Eds.), *Mind, Brain, and Education in Reading Disorders* (pp. 3–15.). New York, NY: Cambridge University Press.

Flegal, K. E., Marin-Gutierrex, A., Ragland, J. D., & Ranganath, C. (2014). Brain mechanisms of successful recognition through retrieval of semantic context. *Journal of Cognitive Neuroscience, 26,* 1694–1704.

Flood, J., Lapp, D., & Fisher, D. (2005). Neurological impress method plus. *Reading Psychology an International Quarterly, 26*(2), 147–160.

Friederici, A. D., & Kotz, S. A. (2003). The brain basis of syntactic processes: Functional imaging and lesion studies. *NeuroImage, 20,* 8–17.

Friederici, A. D., & Weissenborn, J. (2007). Mapping sentence form onto meaning: The syntax-semantic interface. *Brain Research, 1146,* 50–58.

Fry, E. (1998). The most common phonograms. *The Reading Teacher, 51,* 620–622.

Garan, E. M. (2005). Scientific Flimflam: A who's who of entrepreneurial research. In B. Altwerger (Ed.), *Reading for profit: How the bottom line leaves kids behind* (pp. 21–33). Portsmouth, NH: Heinemann.

Gilbert, C. D., & Sigman, M. (2007). Brain states: Top-down influences in sensory processing. *Neuron, 54,* 677–696.

Goldstein, E. B. (2008). *Cognitive psychology: Connecting mind, research, and everyday experience* (2nd ed.). Belmont, CA: Wadsworth.

Goodman, K. (1986). *What's whole in whole language.* Portsmouth, NH: Heinemann Educational Books.

Goodman, Y. M., & Goodman, K. S. (2013). To err is human: Learning about language processes by analyzing miscues. In D. Alvermann, N. J. Unrau,

& R. B. Ruddell (Eds.), *Theoretical models and processes of reading* (pp. 523–543). Newark, DE: International Reading Association.

Graves, D. (1983). *Writing: Teachers and children at work.* Portsmouth, NH: Heinemann.

Graves, M. F., & Silverman, R. (2011). Interventions to enhance vocabulary development. In A. McGill-Franzen & R. L. Allington (Eds.), *Handbook of reading disability research.* New York, NY: Routledge.

Guthrie, J. T., Wigfield, A., Metsala, J. L., & Cox, K. E. (2004). Motivational and cognitive predictors of text comprehension and reading amount. In B. Ruddel & N. Unrau (Eds.) *Theoretical models and processes of reading* (5th ed.) (pp. 929–953). Newark, DE: International Reading Association.

Hamre, B. K., & Pianta, R. C. (2005). Can instructional and emotional support in the first-grade classroom make a difference for children at risk of school failure? *Child Development, 76*(5), 949–967.

Harp, B., & Brewer, J. A. (2005). *The informed reading teacher: Research-based practice.* Upper Saddle River, NJ: Pearson Prentice Hall.

Hawkins, J. (2004). *On intelligence.* New York, NY: Henry Holt.

Helmut, L. (2005). When context hinders! Learn-test compatibility in face recognition. *The Quarterly Journal of Experimental Psychology, 58,* 235–250.

Hinton, C., Miyamota, K., & Dell-Chiese, B. (2008). Brain research, learning and emotions: Implications for education research, policy and practice. *European Journal of Education, 43,* 87–102.

Hogoort, P. (2003). Interplay between syntax and semantics during sentence comprehension: ERP Effects of combining syntactic and semantic violations, *Journal of Cognitive Neuroscience, 15*(6), 883–899.

Houston, D., Al Otaiba, S. A., & Torgesen, J. K. (2006). Learning to read: Phonics and fluency. In D. Browder & F. Spooner (Eds.), *Teaching language arts, math, and science to students with significant cognitive disabilities.* Baltimore, MD: Brookes.

Hruby, G. G. (2009). Grounding reading comprehension in the neuroscience literatures. In S. E. Israel & G. P. Duffy (Eds.), *Handbook of research on reading comprehension* (pp. 189–223). New York, NY: Routledge.

Hruby, G. G., & Goswami, U. (2013). Educational neuroscience for reading researchers. In D. Alvermann, N. J. Unrau, & R. B. Ruddell (Eds.), *Theoretical models and processes of reading* (pp. 558–588). Newark, DE: International Reading Association.

International Reading Association and the National Association for the Education of Young Children (1998). *Learning to reading and write: Developmentally appropriate practices for young children.* Retrieved from www.reading.org/Libraries/position-statements-and-resolutions/ps1027_NAEYC.pdf.

Isakson, R. L., & Miller, J. W. (1976). Sensitivity to syntactic and semantic cues in good and poor comprehenders. *Journal of Educational Psychology, 68,* 787–792.

Jennings, J. H., Caldwell, J. S., & Lerner, J. W. (2010). *Reading problems: Assessment and teaching strategies* (6th ed.). Boston, MA: Allyn & Bacon.

Jensen, E. (2005). *Teaching with the brain in mind* (2nd ed.). Alexandria, VA: Association for Supervision and Curriculum Development.

Johannessen, L. R., & McCann, T. M. (2009). Adolescents who struggle with literacy. In L. Christenbury, R. Bomer, & P. Smagorinsky (Eds.), *Handbook of Adolescent Literacy Research* (pp. 65–79). New York, NY: Guildford Press.

Johnson, A. (1998). Word class: A way to modify spelling instruction for gifted learners. *The Roeper Review, 20,* 128–131.

Johnson, A. (2000). *Up and out: Using thinking skills to enhance learning.* Boston, MA: Allyn & Bacon.

Johnson, A. (2008). *Teaching reading and writing: A guidebook for tutoring and remediating students.* Lanham, MD: Rowman Littlefield Education.

Johnson, A. (2009). *Making connections in elementary and middle school social studies* (2nd ed.). Thousand Oaks, CA: Sage.

Johnson, A. (2012). Affect and adolescents with severe reading disabilities. *Encounter: Education for Meaning and Social Justice, 25*(3), 1–8.

Johnson, A., & Graves, M. (1997). Scaffolding: A tool for enhancing the reading experience of all students. *Texas Journal of Reading, 3,* 23–30.

Julia, E. (2006). Researching children's experience hermeneutically and holistically. *Alberta Journal of Educational Research, 52,* 111–126.

Kennedy, D., & Weener, P. (1974). Visual and auditory training with the cloze procedure to improve reading and listening comprehension. *Reading Research Quarterly, 8,* 524–541.

Koch, C. (2004). *The quest for consciousness: A neurobiological approach.* Englewood, CO: Roberts and Company.

Krashen, S. D. (2004). *The power of reading: Insights from research* (2nd ed.). Portsmouth, NH: Heinemann.

Krashen, S. D. (2011). *Free voluntary reading.* Santa Barbara, CA: Libraries Unlimited.

Kuhn, M. R., & Stahl, S. A. (2013). Fluency: Developmental and remedial practices revisited. In D. Alvermann, N. Unrau, & R. Ruddell (Eds.), *Theoretical models and processes of reading* (6th ed., 385–411). Neward, DE: International Reading Association.

Kuperberg, G. (2007). Neural mechanisms of language comprehension: Challenges to syntax. *Brain Research, 1146,* 23–49.

Lane, H. B., & Allen, S. A. (2010). The vocabulary-rich classroom: Modeling sophisticated word use to promote word consciousness and vocabulary growth. *The Reading Teacher, 63,* 362–370.

LeDoux, J. (1996). *The emotional brain: The mysterious underpinnings of emotional life.* New York, NY: Simon & Schuster.

Lim, J., Reiser, R., & Z. Olina. (2009) The effects of part-task and whole-task instructional approaches on acquisition and transfer of a complex cognitive skill. *Educational Technology Research & Development, 57,* 61–77.

Lipson, M. Y., & Wixson, K. K. (2009). *Assessment & instruction of reading and writing difficulties: An interactive approach* (4th ed.). Boston, MA: Pearson.

Machazo, G. M., & Motz, L. L. (2005). Brain research: Implications to diverse learners. *Science Educator, 14,* 56–60.

Martin, N. M, & Kuke, N. K. (2011). Interventions to enhance informational text comprehension. In A. McGill-Franzen & R. Allington (Eds.), *Handbook of reading disability research* (pp. 345–361). New York, NY: Routledge.

McCormick, S. (2003). *Instructing students who have literacy problems* (4th ed.). Upper Saddle River, NJ: Merrill Prentice Hall.

McCormick S., & Zutell, J. (2011). *Instructing students who have literacy problems* (6th ed.). Boston, MA: Pearson.

McLaughlin, M. (2010). *Content area reading: Teaching and learning in an age of multiple literacies.* Boston, MA: Pearson.

McVee, M. B., Dunsmore, K., & Gauelek, J. (2013). Schema theory revisited. In D. Alvermann, N. J. Unrau, & R. B. Ruddell (Eds.), *Theoretical models and processes of reading* (pp. 489–523). Newark, DE: International Reading Association.

Morrow, L. M., & Dougherty, S. (2011). *Early Literacy development: Merging perspectives that influence practice.* In D. Lapp & D. Fisher (Eds.), *Handbook of research on teaching the English language arts* (3rd ed., pp. 39–52). New York, NY: Routledge.

Münte, T., Heinze, H., & Mangun, G. (1993). Dissociation of brain activity related to syntactic and semantic aspects of language. *Journal of Cognitive Neuroscience, 5,* 335–344.

National Institute for Child Health and Development. (2000). *Report of the National Reading Panel: Teaching children to read.* Bethesda, MD: National Institutes of Health.

Neuman, S. B. (2006). The knowledge gap: Implications for early education. In D. K. Dickenson & S. B. Neuman (Eds.), *Handbook of early literacy research* (Vol. 2, pp. 29–40). New York, NY: Guildford Press.

Ormand, J. E. (2012). *Human learning* (6th ed.). Boston, MA: Pearson.

Osterhout, L., & Holcomb, P. J. (1992). Event-related brain potentials elicited by syntactic anomaly. *Journal of Memory and Language, 31,* 785–806.

Paciga, K., Hoffman, J. L., & Teale, W. H. (2011). The national early literacy panel and preschool literacy instruction: Greenlights, caution lights, and red lights. *Young Children, 66,* 49–57.

Paulson, E. J. (2008). Miscues and eye movement: Functions of comprehension. In A. Flurky, E. Paulson, & K. Goodman (Eds.), *Scientific realism in studies of reading* (pp. 247–264). New York, NY: Lawrence Erlbaum Associates.

Paulson, E., & Freeman, A. (2003). *Insight from the eyes: The science of effective reading instruction.* Portsmouth, NH: Heinemann.

Paulson, E. J., & Goodman, K. S. (2008). Re-reading eye-movement research: Support for transactional models of reading. In A. Flurky, E. Paulson, & K. Goodman (Eds.), *Scientific Realism in Studies of Reading* (pp. 25–50). New York, NY: Lawrence Erlbaum Associates.

Pearson, P. D., & Hiebert, E. H. (2013). National reports in literacy: Building a scientific base for practice and policy. In D. Alvermann, N. J. Unrau, & R. B. Ruddell (Eds.), *Theoretical models and processes of reading* (6th ed., pp. 1133–1149). Newark, DE: International Reading Association.

Piaget, J., & Inhelder, B. (1969). *The psychology of the child.* New York, NY: Basic Books.

Poldrack, R. A., Wagner, A. D., Prull, M. W., Desmond, J. E., Glover, G. H., & Gabrieli, D. E. (1999). Functional specialization for semantic and phonological processing in the left inferior prefrontal cortex. *NeuroImage, 10,* 15–35.

Rasinski, T. V., Padak, N. D., & Fawett, G. (2010). *Teaching children who find reading difficult.* Boston, MA: Pearson.

Rayner, K. (2009). Eye movements and attention in reading, scene perception, and visual search. *The Quarterly Journal of Experimental Psychology, 62,* 1457–1506.

Rayner, K., & Well, A. D. (1996). Effects of contextual constraint on eye movements in reading: A further examination. *Psychonomic Bulletin & Review, 3,* 504–509.

Rayner, K., Juhasz, B., & Pollatsek, A. (2007). Eye movements during reading. In M. Snowling & C. Hulme (Eds.), *The science of reading: A handbook* (pp. 79–97). Malden, MA: Blackwell.

Rayner, K., Liversedge, S. P., White, S. J., & Vergilino-Perez, D. (2003). Reading disappearing text: Cognitive control of eye movements. *Psychological Science, 14,* 385–388.

Reutzel, D. R., & Cooter, R. B. (1996). *Teaching children to read.* Englewood Cliffs, NJ: Prentice Hall.

Roger, R. W., Peck, S. C., & Nasir, N. S. (2006). Self and identity processes in school motivation, learning, and achievement. In P. Alexander & P. Winne (Eds.), *Handbook of Educational Psychology* (pp. 391–424). Mahwah, NJ: Lawrence Erlbaum Associates.

Rosenblatt, L. M. (1983). *Literature as exploration* (4th ed.). New York, NY: Modern Language Association.

Sakai, K. L., Noguchi, Y., Takeuchi, T., & Watanabe, E. (2002). Selective priming of syntactic processing by event-related transcranial magnetic stimulation of Broca's areas. *Neuron, 35,* 1177–1182.

Schraw, G. (2006). Knowledge: Structures and processes. In P. Alexander & P. Winne (Eds.), *Handbook of educational psychology* (2nd ed., pp. 245–263). Mahway, NJ: Lawrence Erlbaum Associates.

Schulz, E., Maurer, U., van der Mark, S., Bucher, K., Brem, S., Martain, E., & Brandeis, D., (2008). Impaired semantic processing during sentence reading in children with dyslexia: Combined fMRI and ERP evidence. *NeuroImage, 41,* 153–168.

Schunk, D. H., & Zimmerman, B. J. (2006). Competence and control beliefs: Distinguishing the means and ends. In P. Alexander & P. Winne (Eds.), *Handbook of Educational Psychology* (2nd ed., pp. 349–368). Mahwah, NJ: Lawrence Erlbaum Associates.

Schwartz, J. M., & Begley, S. (2002). *The mind and the brain: Neuroplasticity and the power of mental force.* New York, NY: Regan Books.

Sherman, S. M., & Guillery, R. W. (2004). The visual relays in the thalamus. In L. M. Chalupa & J. S. Werner (Eds.), *The Visual Neurosciences* (pp. 565–591). Cambridge: MIT Press.

Siegel, D. J. (2007). *The mindful brain.* New York, NY: W. W. Norton & Company.

Smith, F. (2003). *Unspeakable acts, unnatural practices: Flaws and fallacies in "scientific" reading instruction.* Portsmouth, NH: Heinemann.

Sousa, D. A. (2011). *How the brain learns* (4th ed.). Thousand Oaks, CA: Corwin.

Sousa, D. A. (2012). *How the brain learns* (4th ed). Thousand Oaks, CA: Corwin.

Sousa, D. A. (2014). *How the brain learns to read* (2nd ed.). Thousand Oaks, CA: Corwin.

Stahl, S. (1999). *Vocabulary development*. Brookline, MA: Brookline Books.

Sternberg, R. (2009). *Cognitive psychology* (5th ed.). Belmont, CA: Wadsworth.

Sternberg, R. J., & Williams, W. M. (2009). *Educational Psychology* (2nd ed.). Boston, MA: Allyn & Bacon.

Stetter, M. E., & Hughes, M. T. (2010). Using story grammar to assist students with learning disabilities and reading difficulties improve their comprehension. *Education and Treatment of Children, 33*(1), 115–151.

Strauss, S. L. (2011). Neuroscience and dyslexia. In A. McGill-Franzen & R. L. Allington (Eds.), *Handbook of reading disability research* (pp. 79–90). New York, NY: Routledge.

Strauss, S. L., Goodman, K. S., & Paulson, E. J. (2009). Brain research and reading: How emerging concepts in neuroscience support a meaning construction view of the reading process. *Education Research and Review, 4*(2), 21–33.

Swanson, E. A., & Vaugh, S. (2010). An observation study of reading instruction provided to elementary students with learning disabilities in the resource room. *Psychology in the Schools, 47*, 481–491.

Tanaka, J. W., & Gauthier, I. (1997). Expertise in object and face recognition. In R. L. Goldstone, P. G. Schyns, & D. L. Medin (Eds.), *Psychology of learning and motivation, mechanisms of perceptual learning* (Vol. 36, pp. 83–125). San Diego, CA: Academic Press.

Taylor, B., Anderson, R., Au, K., & Raphael, T. (2000). Discretion in the transition of reading research to policy. *Educational Researcher, 29*, 16–26.

Teale, W. H., Hoffman, J. L., & Paciga, K. A. (2010). Where is NELP leading preschool literacy instruction? Potential positives and pitfalls. *Educational Researcher, 39*, 311–315.

Tompkins, G. E. (2011). *Literacy in the early grades: A successful start for preK–4 readers and writers* (3rd ed.). Boston, MA: Pearson.

Trueswell, J. C. 1996. The role of lexical frequency in syntactic ambiguity resolution. *Journal of Memory and Language, 35*, 566–585.

Van Berkum, J., Hagoort, P., & Brown, C. (1999) Semantic integration in sentences and discourse: Evidence from the N400. *Journal of Cognitive Neuroscience, 11*, 657–671.

Van Ryzin, M. J. (2011). Motivation and reading disabilities. In A. McGill-Franzen & R. L. Allington (Eds.), *Handbook of Reading Disability Research* (pp. 242–253). New York, NY: Routledge.

Vygotsky, L. S. (1962). Thought and language. Cambridge: MIT Press.

Vygotsky, L. S. (1978). *Mind in society: The development of higher psychological processes*. Cambridge, MA: Harvard University Press.

Vygotsky, L. S. (1981). *Mind in society: The development of higher psychological processes*. Cambridge, MA: Harvard University Press.

Wagner, R. K., & Stanovich, K. E. (1996). Expertise in reading. In K. A. Ericson (Ed.), *The road to excellence: The acquisition of expert performance in the arts and sciences, sports, and games* (pp. 189–226). Mahwah, NJ: Lawrence Erlbaum Associates.

Weaver, C. (2009). *Reading process*. Portsmouth, NH: Heinemann.

Weaver, P. (1979). Improving reading instruction: Effects of sentence organization instruction. *Reading Research Quarterly, 15,* 127–146.

Wharton-McDonald, R. (2011). Expert classroom instruction for students with reading disabilities. In A. McGill-Franzen & R. S. Allington (Eds.), *Handbook of reading disability research* (pp. 265–272). New York, NY: Routledge.

White, T. G., Sowell, J., & Yanagihara, A. (1989). Teaching elementary students to use word-part clues. *The Reading Teacher, 42,* 302–308.

Wigfield, A., Byrnes, J., & Eccles, J. (2006). Development during early and middle adolescence. In P. Alexander & P. Winne (Eds.), *Handbook of Educational Psychology* (pp. 87–114). Mahwah, NJ: Lawrence Erlbaum Associates.

Xu J., Kemeny, S., Park, G., Frattali, C., & Bran, A. (2005). Language in context: Emergent features of word, sentence, and narrative comprehension. *Neuroimage, 25,* 1002–1015.

Yaden, D. B., Rowe, D. W., & MacGillivray, L. M. (2000). Emergent literacy: A matter (polyphony) of perspectives. In M. Kamil, P. Mosenthal, P. Pearson, & R. Baar (Eds.), *Handbook of reading research: Volume III* (pp. 425–454). New York, NY: Routledge.

Zeelenberg, R., Pecher, D., Shiffrin, R. M., & Raaijmakers, J. (2003). Semantic context effects and priming in word association. *Psychonomic Bulletin & Review, 10,* 653–660.

Index

A SAGE Company

CORWIN HAS ONE MISSION: to enhance education through intentional professional learning.

We build long-term relationships with our authors, educators, clients, and associations who partner with us to develop and continuously improve the best evidence-based practices that establish and support lifelong learning.

Solutions you want. Experts you trust. Results you need.